Treasures of the
HERMITAGE

Treasures of the

HERMITAGE

by Vitaly Suslov

Newsweek / New York

Editorial Director:
Henry A. La Farge

Introduction by:
Vitaly Suslov

Commentary texts by:
T. Arapova, O. Androsov, V. Berezina, N. Biryukova, A. Bank,
S. Vsevolozhskaya, I. Grigorieva, T. Grek, Yu. Zek, A. Ivanov,
A. Kakovkin, L. Kagane, Yu. Kagan, N. Kosareva, E. Kozhina,
A. Kostenevich, T. Kustodieva, A. Kantor-Gukovskaya, Yu. Kuznetsov,
M. Krzhizhanovskaya, I. Linnik, V. Lukonin, B. Marshak, E. Moiseyenko,
I. Nemilova, N. Nikulin, I. Novoselskaya, O. Neverov, L. Nikiforova,
G. Printseva, E. Renne, I. Saverkina, T. Fomicheva.

Photography:
L. Bogdanov, R. Kirillov, V. Strekalov, L. Kheifets.

Editor:
M. Grigorieva.

Translation:
Daryl Hislop, Miriam Atlas.

Editorial Assistant:
Mary A. La Farge

Published by

NEWSWEEK, INC.
& ARNOLD MONDADORI EDITORE

This volume is being published simultaneously under the
title of *Hermitage/Leningrad*

ISBN 0-88225-301-8
Library of Congress 80-81382 .

INTRODUCTION

Vitaly Suslov,
Sub-Director of the Hermitage

The Hermitage State Museum is one of the greatest in the world. Its history began in the middle of the 18th century with Catherine II's purchase of several pictures by Flemish and Dutch painters from a Berlin merchant called Gotzkowsky in payment of his debt to the Russian Treasury. Brought in 1764 to the shores of the Neva, they were used to decorate several rooms in the newly built Imperial Winter Palace. Thus, almost by chance, the Hermitage collection was begun.

Today the Hermitage buildings spread along the banks of the Neva for almost a kilometer, incorporating almost four hundred rooms, with about three million works of art from different civilizations, epochs, states and peoples. At one time the Empress Catherine II, not without a certain coquettishness, wrote to the French encyclopaedist Grimm: "Only the mice and I admire my treasures." Today, more than three and a half million people come to this unique museum to see these priceless treasures every year.

Although for a century and a half, right up until the October Revolution of 1917, the Hermitage remained strictly a court museum, closed to the man in the street, it developed hand in hand with Russian culture, reflecting the history of its people. The whole collection, the way it grew up, and the speed at which it grew pointed not so much to the tastes and fashions of the time as to historical progress and the demands of Russian society and culture. The rooms of the imperial Hermitage were visited by more than one generation of Russian artists, writers, scholars, art critics and social activists, searching for inspiration among the masterpieces of world art. This should not be seen in any way as contempt for their own national art, but rather as an appreciation of Russian culture as a constituent part of European, and in a wider context, of world culture, and the desire to become acquainted with its greatest achievements.

The story of the Hermitage after the Revolution illustrates particularly well people's awareness of the importance of our artistic heritage. Since that time the Hermitage's collection has grown more than threefold, and the former Imperial Winter Palace with all its treasures has become part of the museum which opens its doors to tens of thousands of visitors every day. The Hermitage is not just a museum in the traditional sense of the word. It does not take long to realize that it is something special. Of course, first and foremost, it is a superb collection of works of art from all over the world. But history has also left its mark here, in rooms that carefully preserve the memory of those events which took place that October night in 1917, when the people in revolt stormed the palace, the last bastion of the bourgeois antipopular government, and seized it. Nor should it be forgotten that the Hermitage as a whole, including the interior, is an outstanding example of 18th- to 19th-century Russian architecture, the work of many Russian architects. Today the Hermitage is a leading scientific and educational center. Like its sister museums, the Louvre and the Metropolitan, the immense holdings of the Hermitage provide a complete picture of the history of civilization, allowing the visitor to see the path trodden by man in his artistic quest throughout the ages.

The Hermitage's collection of Western European art, especially the old masters, is largely responsible for the museum's worldwide renown. However, among its other collections are many pieces of no less importance from other civilizations, which should not be ignored. The archeological collections contain the earliest objects in the museum, and these are constantly being added to every year from expeditions to different regions of the Soviet Union. Among the extensive holdings of the Department of Prehistoric Cultures, for instance, the visitor can see examples of sculptural art found on Palaeolithic sites, as well as objects made during the Stone, Bronze and Early Iron ages in Siberia, Central Asia, the Northern Caucasus and the European part of the U.S.S.R.

Famous throughout the world are the Scythian antiquities, the art of the nomadic peoples who inhabited the vast spaces of Eastern Europe and Asia between the Danube and Mongolia in the 1st millennium B.C. These artifacts comprise primarily goldwork of great originality— pieces of jewelry, objects for domestic and religious use, costume decorations, horse harnesses and weapons. Born of the barbaric life on the steppes and influenced by the advanced civilizations of Asia Minor and Greece, this art is astonishing in the fantasy and refinement of its distinctive animal-style. The Hermitage possesses the largest collection in the world of the culture of these ancient nomadic peoples, primarily from the tombs of tribal chieftains—the so-called royal tumuli—in southern Ukraine, Northern Caucasus and the Altai.

The cultures of the nomadic and settled peoples who occupied Russian soil in primitive times cannot be said truly to represent the immediate antecedents and base of Russian art properly speaking. Nevertheless, these cultures undoubtedly had some influence on the development of Russian decorative and applied art, especially as regards ornament.

The Hermitage offers the opportunity of tracing the development of Russian culture, its character, and special traits. As regards this specific part of the collections, one must bear in mind that when the Russian Museum was founded in 1898, practically all the Russian paintings were transferred there, away from the Hermitage. The makeup of the Hermitage's collection was in turn altered by the addition to it of the Winter Palace's treasures, which consisted for the most part of decorative and applied arts, historic and cultural objects, to which were added the collections from the Museum of Russian Life. Thus although today we can speak of a relatively good collection of paintings (including icons), graphic art, and certain first rate examples of sculpture, the most important aspect of this part of the Hermitage is the extraordinary richness of every kind of Russian decorative art from the 12th century through to the beginning of the 20th. This includes costume, furniture, tapestries, textiles, lace, engraved gems, porcelain and glass from all the Russian workshops, as well as silver, jewelry, chandeliers, candelabra, and every kind of peasant craftsmanship.

The peoples of Soviet Transcaucasia and Central Asia—on whose territories in ancient times and in the early Middle Ages different autonomous states arose, starting with the ancient kingdom of Urartu (on the territory of today's Armenia)—also have a rich history behind them. Their unique cultures are represented in the extensive collections of the Department of the Soviet East and of the Far East. These collections are wide-ranging both in the period of time they cover, and in the variety of cultures they represent. They encompass a period extending from the 4th century B.C. to the 20th, and a geographic area stretching from the

Near East, Asia Minor, and Central Asia to the Far East.

The collections of ancient Egyptian, Sumerian, Babylonian, Assyrian, and Far Eastern art contain examples which range from monumental low reliefs to the most delicate jewelry. The extraordinary importance which the ancient civilizations of the Near and Far East have in the history of human cultures is represented in the Hermitage by collections which rank among the finest in the world. It is sufficient only to mention the remarkably complete collections of the Chinese decorative arts (lacquers, enamels, porcelains, jades, textiles). Equally impressive are the holdings of Persian toreutics, especially the Sassanian silver, and one of the most important collections in the world of ivory carvings and silver. There are also Byzantine icons, monumental frescoes from medieval sites in Central Asia, sculptures and paintings from Tibet and elsewhere. Not to be overlooked are the collections of the medieval and contemporary arts of Japan, India, Indonesia, Turkey, the Soviet Republics of Transcaucasia and Central Asia.

The earliest of the Hermitage's collections is that of classical antiquities. The first ancient marbles were acquired as long ago as the beginning of the 18th century by Peter I. They include the celebrated *Taurida Venus,* a Roman copy of a 3rd-century B.C. Greek original. From the second half of the 18th century onward, the Hermitage's collection of antiquities expanded at a fast pace, thanks in large measure to the excavations then taking place in Italy. This collection is still being constantly added to, through the continuing work of Soviet archeologists on the ancient sites of Greek colonies in the northern Black Sea coastlands. Outside of Greece and Italy, the Hermitage's collection of classical antiquities is now probably the largest in the world. There are literally dozens of rooms in the museum dedicated to Roman portraits, vases, sculpture, bronzes, carved and engraved gems, and jewelry. The huge numismatic collection—among the largest in the world—and what amounts to a veritable arsenal of decorated arms and armor help give an overall picture of the enormous wealth of the Hermitage today.

It must, however, be acknowledged that the fame of the Hermitage rests largely upon its remarkable collections of Western European art: paintings, sculptures, drawings, and the decorative and applied arts. Practically every European school is represented, with works of the most famous artists, and every aspect of the decorative arts. The most completely represented in the number of works on view is the French school. Outside of France itself, there is no other museum to rival this one, not only as regards paintings, but also, to no lesser degree, sculpture, graphics and the decorative arts.

The most important movement in French art of the 17th century was Classicism, whose leading exponents, Nicolas Poussin and Claude Lorrain, are each represented by a good dozen of famous canvases. The 17th century did, however, produce other movements in painting, and these are also fairly well represented. Alongside the genre paintings of the Le Nain brothers—fascinating in their authentic portrayal of the humble life—can be seen historical paintings of the academic movement by artists such as Simon Vouet and Charles Lebrun, and the work of the great portrait painter Nicolas Largillière, in the second half of the century.

The collection of French 18th-century paintings consists of about 300 canvases and includes the names of all the leading artists. Antoine Watteau is represented by no less than six works, among which are the *Savoyard with a Marmot, Actors of the Théâtre Français,* and *A Capricious Woman,* all representing high points of his development as an artist. Equally comprehensive is the collection of works by Boucher and Lancret. There are characteristic works by Chardin and Fragonard, and entire rooms devoted to Jean-Baptiste Greuze and Hubert Robert. Eighteenth-century portraiture is represented by Nattier and Tocqué.

The collection of French painting from the first half of the 19th century is not so well endowed, although all the leading artists are represented by at least one or two works. On the other hand, the period from the second half of the 19th century to the beginning of the present century is represented by superb examples. There are ten canvases by Claude Monet which demonstrate his continuous experimentation, from the early *Lady in the Garden* to the late series of *London Fogs.* Together with works by Renoir, Pissarro and Degas, they show the problems which faced the Impressionists and the artistic solutions which they found to resolve them. The collection of works illustrating subsequent movements in French art is just as great, both in quantity and significance. There are four van Gogh canvases from his late, mature period, and eleven Cézanne canvases showing different aspects of his achievements—in portraiture, still life and landscape. Notable also are the works by Gauguin, Matisse and Picasso. There are fifteen canvases by Gauguin, all dating from his Tahitian period, when he was at the height of his powers. The thirty-five canvases by Matisse (including *The Dance, Music, Red Room,* and *The Family Group*), are mostly from the period between 1900 and 1913. The thirty-one Picassos are also from about the same period, beautifully illustrating his "Blue" and "Pink" periods and in particular his experiments with Cubism. One should mention likewise the selection of works by Derain, Bonnard, Vuillard, Marquet, van Dongen and Maurice Denis.

The first paintings by Italian artists to come to the Hermitage were from the famous Crozat Collection, bought in Paris in 1772. Today the Italian paintings occupy no less than thirty-seven rooms. The early period is the least well represented, although among the works from the first half of the 14th century can be seen that exquisite Simone Martini panel of the *Annunciation* (which is actually only half of the original diptych). On the other hand, the 15th-century section yields a whole gallery of famous names—the Florentines Filippo Lippi, Fra Angelico, Sandro Botticelli, Filippino Lippi; the Venetian Cima da Conegliano; the Ferrarese painter Lorenzo Costa; and the Umbrian Pietro Perugino.

The collection of High Renaissance paintings is of particular value. It is headed by two Leonardo da Vinci masterpieces, the *Madonna with a Flower* (the *Benois Madonna*) and the *Litta Madonna.* They are surrounded by a precious group of works by Leonardo's followers—Andrea del Sarto, Cesare da Sesto, Bernardino Luini, Francesco Melzi, to which can be added the Parmesan painter Correggio.

Among the Hermitage's prized possessions also are two masterpieces by Raphael: his early *Conestabile Madonna* and the more mature *Holy Family with the Beardless Joseph.* As far as the rest of the High Renaissance is concerned, the Venetian School is the most important. Here we find Giorgione's *Judith,* eight canvases by Titian, five by Veronese, six large decorative panels by Tiepolo, landscapes by Canaletto and Guardi.

Equally wide-ranging is the collection of Italian Baroque, as regards both the various local schools of the 17th and 18th centuries and the work of their leading masters. These include such artists as the Genoese painters Strozzi, Magnasco, Castiglione, the Neapolitans Salvator Rosa, Luca Giordano, Torelli, the Bolognese Crespi. One of the major masterpieces of the Hermitage is Caravaggio's *The Lute Player.*

Renowned throughout the world both for their size and comprehensiveness are the Hermitage's Dutch and Flemish collections, which number about fifteen hundred pictures. The leading master of the Flemish school, Rubens, is represented by twenty-two canvases of different types—large compositions on mythological subjects, landscapes, portraits, and nineteen sketches for some of his famous paintings (such as *The Lion Hunt,* now in the Alte Pinakothek, Munich), and studies for the decorations marking the Spanish ruler's festive entry into Antwerp. The van Dyck collection is likewise very rich, comprising twenty-five portraits, including those from his London period. The panorama of 17th-century Flemish art is rounded out by the works of such masters as Jordaens, Snyder, Brouwer and David Teniers, each of whom is represented by superlative examples.

Dutch art has long enjoyed particular attention inside Russia. Paintings by Dutch artists figured largely among the "foreign" works of art acquired by Peter I during his travels in Europe, and the first consignment of pictures to arrive in the Winter Palace from Berlin in 1764 consisted mostly of Dutch works. It is therefore not surprising that the Hermitage's holdings of Dutch painting, being very extensive, enable the visitor to trace the development of all the different types in the school with outstanding examples. Among its leading landscapists are Jan van Goyen, Solomon van Ruysdael, Aert van der Neer, and the more romantic Jacob van Ruysdael; animalistic genre is represented by Paulus Potter and Aelbert Cuyp; while still life in its wealth of forms and colors is to be found in the famous "breakfasts" and "desserts" of William Claesz Heda, Pieter Claesz and Willem Kalf. In the vast portrait gallery are two splendid works by Frans Hals; and finally the painting of everyday life, costume and genre is represented by artists such as Adriaen van Ostade, Jan Steen, Pieter de Hooch and Gerard Terborch.

The most celebrated works in the Dutch collection are the twenty-six Rembrandt canvases, which include every stage of the master's development, and every aspect of his oeuvre. Such canvases as *Flora, Danaé, Portrait of an Old Man in Red, The Holy Family, David and Uriah, Return of the Prodigal Son* are only a partial list of masterpieces which hold such pride of place in the Hermitage.

The collection of Spanish paintings is not nearly as large (about two hundred canvases), but very high in quality. Works by Luis de Morales, Juan Pantoja de La Cruz, the great El Greco's *The Apostles Peter and Paul,* all characterize the art, the ideals and the spirit of 16th-century Spain. But the 17th century—the "Golden Age" of Spanish art—is better and more extensively represented. The visitor here encounters a constellation of great names: Velázquez, Ribera, Zurbarán, Murillo. The two Velázquez paintings are surrounded by the works of his pupils and followers, Juan Pareja, Antonio Puga and Antonio de Pereda. There are twenty Murillos—including both religious and genre themes. Ribera and Zurbarán are represented by highly characteristic works.

The English and German collections are also notable, although not as complete as previously mentioned collections, nor on the same level of importance. The five works by Lucas Cranach the Elder undoubtedly rank among the finest examples of German Renaissance art. Sixteenth-century portraiture is represented with works by Ambrosius Holbein, Barthel Bruyn the Elder, Nicholas Neufchatel and others. As regards the 18th century—the period of Neoclassicism in Germany—it is necessary only to mention the works of two of the most popular artists of the period, Anton Mengs and Angelica Kauffmann. German Romanticism of the first half of the 19th century is represented by superb examples of the work of Caspar David Friedrich.

The collecting of English paintings in the Hermitage began by the Russian court placing orders with London artists, in particular Joshua Reynolds, president of the Royal Academy. English painting was at its height in the 18th century, and this is the period which is best represented in the Hermitage. It boasts not only Reynolds, but his disciple George Romney, also the eminent portrait and landscape painter Thomas Gainsborough, the portraitists Henry Raeburn and John Hoppner, the genre and landscape painter George Morland. The English school is rounded out by three well-known artists from the first half of the 19th century: Thomas Lawrence, George Dawe and Richard Parkes Bonington.

Only the largest sections of paintings have so far been discussed, although the Hermitage does possess examples of many more national schools, for instance, the socialist countries of Eastern Europe, Scandinavia and the Americas.

The policy of the Hermitage is to have on permanent display as many different types of art as possible—painting, sculpture, decorative and applied art—while the graphic arts are shown in special temporary exhibitions. This makes it possible to get an overall impression of the style of each epoch, to get the true feeling of its character, for a deeper understanding of the various trends of creative activity. The storerooms of the Hermitage are so rich that it is possible to mount fully comprehensive exhibitions covering any school or movement.

The Hermitage's collection of Western European sculpture, comprising about 2,000 works, is one of the largest in the world. Besides comprehensive displays there are special groups, such as the Rodin room and the room of Italian 18th- and early 19th-century marbles. The first consignment of Western European sculpture to arrive in the Hermitage came at the end of the 18th century as part of the Lyde-Brown collection, which was assembled in Italy. This collection included two High Renaissance masterpieces, Michelangelo's *Crouching Boy* and Lorenzo Lorenzetto's *Dead Boy on a Dolphin* (after a sketch by Raphael). To this day Italian sculpture forms the major part of the Hermitage's sculptural holdings. The earliest works date from the 15th century, including marbles by Antonio Rossellino, glazed terra-cottas by Luca and Andrea della Robbia, portraits by Savelli Sperando and Benedetto da Maiano. Of particular importance is the group of bronzes by Michelangelo's contemporaries and followers, Bandinelli, Sansovino, Cellini and others. The Baroque style, so powerfully developed in Italian sculpture, is represented in the Hermitage by two magnificent Bernini terra-cotta models (*Self Portrait* and the *Ecstasy of St. Theresa*) and a very typical work by Mazzuoli, *The Death of Adonis.*

But the most extensive group of Italian sculptures in the Hermitage is from the Neoclassical period, with works dating from the end of the 18th to the beginning of the 19th centuries. Canova, the outstanding master of the movement, is represented by many famous works, including *Cupid and Psyche,* the *Penitent Magdalene, The Dancer* and others. In this section there are also Neoclassical works by northern European artists living in Rome at that time. Among these, the first name to spring to mind is the Dane, Thorwaldsen, who is represented by a number of works.

Equally important is the Hermitage's collection of French sculpture, presenting the varied characteristics and kinds from the 14th to the 20th centuries. While there are only a few pieces from the French Renaissance, the later periods are more fully represented. The 18th century in France in particular was a period of great activity in the plastic arts, a development which is beautifully demonstrated in the Hermitage's rooms with works by Caffieri, Gillet, Houdon, Falconet.

The second half of the 19th century and the beginning of the 20th mark a memorable page in the history of French sculpture. One name which stands out is Jules Dalou, famous for his huge compositions and for his profound psychological portraits which reflect a transition to the spirit of modern research. The new age itself produced Auguste Rodin, for whose works a special room is reserved, in which are exhibited sculptures of various periods of his creative life, from the original plaster of *Bronze Age,* given by the sculptor to the St. Petersburg Academy in 1877, to the small mask of the Japanese Dancer Khanako, produced in 1901. The great bronzes of Rodin's pupil, Eugène Bourdelle, *Eloquence, Beethoven, Bust of Rodin* and the bronzes of Maillol and Matisse show the trends of French sculpture after Rodin. In connection with the European schools of plastic art, one should not overlook the interesting collections of Dutch and German sculpture, mostly of the 15th to 16th centuries.

Western European drawings in the Hermitage, which number in the tens of thousands, rival any other collection in the world. First place here, of course, goes to the Italian, French and Flemish schools. The Italian 16th century is represented by many artists. The Florentine and Roman schools for example are represented by Primaticcio, the Zuccari brothers, Piero di Cosimo, Giulio Romano, de Roberti, Salviati. The Venetian section comprises works by Titian, Tintoretto and Veronese. There are almost two hundred sketches by Giovanni Battista and Domenico Tiepolo, and many also by Guardi, Canaletto and other 18th-century masters.

As regards the holdings of French drawings, the Hermitage can match any collection in France. This is especially true of the magnificent group of 16th-century pencil portraits, notably those of François Clouet and Pierre Dumoustier. There are also many interesting sketches and studies for compositions and landscapes by Nicolas Poussin and Claude Lorrain, works by Jean Bellange, Claude Mellan, Lagneau and others active in the 17th century. The 18th century in France saw the development of drawing as an independent art form. All the leading painters, Watteau, Boucher, Greuze, Fragonard, Lancret, were also excellent graphic artists, and the Hermitage possesses some of the outstanding examples of their work. The 19th century does not fare so well, being represented by only a limited number of artists, such as Ingres and Edouard Manet.

Flemish graphic art is well represented, with examples of all the major artists in the varied aspects of this school. The collection includes studies and original landscapes and portraits by Rubens, a magnificent watercolor by Jordaens, and sketches for paintings and portraits by van Dyck. Works by Fyt, Cuellinius, van Diepenbeeck, van Orley round out the panorama of Flemish drawing.

Among the works of artists of other schools mention should be made of numerous sheets by the Dutch artists Bloemaert and Goltzius, pen-and-ink landscapes and red chalk studies by Rembrandt, a large crayon drawing by Dürer, drawings by his contemporaries Hans Holbein the Elder, Altdorfer and others.

The Hermitage's holdings of decorative and applied art are also on a par with any in Europe—comparable to those of the Louvre and London's Victoria and Albert Museum. Although perhaps not as extensive, they include superb examples of Romanesque and Gothic art, from the 9th century onward. The successive phases in the development of European decorative art are represented in the Hermitage as comprehensively as possible. The porcelain collection, comprised of more than 14,000 pieces, contains examples of all the European wares. The situation is the same as regards majolica (the earliest pieces dating from 12th-century Spain), glass (dating back to 15th-century Venetian glass), silver (the earliest being pieces from Nüremberg and Augsburg dating from the 16th century), Limoges enamels, and jewelry. Among the best in Europe is the collection of German, French and Flemish tapestries, comprising some 300 examples dating from the 15th century onward. The sheer number of items in the Hermitage's collections of decorative arts testifies to the breadth and historical importance of the holdings: 3,000 pieces of furniture (from the 15th century onward), 5,000 specimens of textiles and embroidery (from the 14th century), 1,500 examples of lace, 10,500 carved and engraved gems, intaglios, etc.

The Hermitage State Museum constitutes a whole world in itself—a huge, diversified universe of forms, colors and images which bring into focus in one continuous record the progression of time and generations. It is a world of dreams and aspirations, open not only to those who want to know about the past, but also to those seeking paths of new life into the future.

GREEK, ROMAN, NEAR EASTERN ART

500 B.C.—XIV century

GREEK ART: PAN PAINTER. *Artemis and a Swan.*

The Pan Master is one of the most subtle and refined artists of the beginning of the 5th century B.C. For his works he chose unusual subjects, some of which remain mysteriously obscure. Among them is the subject of this painting, which is ambiguous as to whether the goddess is feeding or caressing the swan.

The elongated figure of Artemis harmonizes organically with the elegant shape of the lekythos. The clear-cut folds of her drapery graphically underline the vertical structure of the composition. Artemis' face, her headdress, her quiver are drawn with great precision. The figures of the goddess and

GREEK ART: PAN PAINTER
Lekythos with Artemis and a Swan
Attica, ca. 490 B.C.
Terra-cotta; height 14¹⁵⁄₁₆″

p. 19
CHARINOS
Oenochoe in the Form of a Woman's Head
End of VI century B.C.
Painted terra-cotta; height 10⅝″
From Athens

of the swan stand out almost as if in relief against the white background
of the vase. Contributing to this effect also is the black lacquer in the lower
part of the lekythos and the ornamental design on the neck of the vase.

CHARINOS. *Oenochoe in the Form of a Woman's Head.* *p. 19*
Vases in human shape are characteristic of every period of the development
of Greek ceramics. This oenochoe (a pitcher for pouring wine) in the form
of a woman's head is a masterpiece of this type. The modeling of the face
with almond-shaped eyes, the prominent nose, the "archaic" smile, and the
treatment of the hair are stylistically close to sculptures of the Archaic Pe-

riod, in particular to the Korai maidens of the Acropolis. On the large handle is inscribed the signature, "made by Charinos." This oenochoe is one of four signed vases by the Attic ceramist Charinos. Another oenochoe, practically an exact replica of this one, was unearthed in the same tomb and is today in the Berlin State Museums.

GREEK ART
Aphrodite-shaped Vessel
Athens, end of V century B.C.
Painted terra-cotta; height 6⅛"

LEAGROS GROUP. *Black-figure Hydria with Achilles and
the Body of Hector.*   *p. 20*
The artist has chosen an episode from the Iliad as subject for the decoration of this vessel for pouring water: Achilles' victory over Hector, and his abuse of the body of the defeated, which he is attaching to his chariot to be dragged. The vitality of Achilles' figure contrasts with Hector's lifeless body. As if to emphasize the hero's swiftness, the artist has represented on Achilles' helmet an equally swift animal, a fox.
The composition of the painting is precise and balanced. It may possibly derive from some monumental sculpture on the same subject.

ART OF MAGNA GRAECIA. *Athlete.*   *p. 21*
A tall candelabra-like support is crowned by this statuette of an athlete, who originally held in his right hand an object which was probably an ointment jar.
The particular treatment of the muscles, the shape of the ears, and the asymmetric arrangement of the eyebrows associate this bronze with the centers of Magna Graecia and in particular with work from Lokri. However, some people believe the piece is of Attic origin.

GREEK ART. *Aphrodite-shaped Vessel.*   *p. 23*
This little vase in the shape of the goddess Aphrodite is a typical figural vessel of Greek ceramics. The goddess of love and of beauty is depicted at her birth from the sea-foam as she comes out of an opening shell.
The painted surface of the vessel, which is almost perfectly preserved, shows the richness of its original colors. This is particularly valuable since it provides an idea of what Greek sculpture was like in the 5th and 4th centuries B.C., often colored by the foremost painters.

HELLENISTIC ART. *Aphrodite and Eros.*   *p. 24*
Terra-cotta figurines were extremely widespread in Antiquity. They served as gift-offerings to a deity, accompanied the dead to their graves, and later were used as decorations in Greek homes. This accounts for their themes being so varied. Originally they were representations of deities, but in due course genre motifs penetrated the terra-cotta art form. Thanks to this, the Tanagra terra-cotta figurines provide us with rich material for knowledge of the way of life and customs of the ancient Greeks.
In this statuette, even Aphrodite is represented as a thoughtful mother playing with a small child. Only the wings on Eros' back remind us that we are looking at a goddess.

HELLENISTIC ART. *Woman with a Lekythos.* •   *p. 25*
The terra-cotta figurines from the Greek town of Tanagra occupy a very special place in small-scale classical Greek plastic art. The female figures depicted in different poses are characterized by a certain grace and expres-

HELLENISTIC ART
Eros and Aphrodite
End of the IV century B.C.
Terra-cotta; height 3⅜″
From Tanagra (Boeotia)

siveness of movement, and the irresistible attraction of youth. The development of the Hellenistic figurine was greatly influenced by the leading sculptors of the 4th century B.C., in particular Praxiteles. His influence is especially evident in the figurine *Woman with a Lekythos*. The artist has conformed strictly to the rules laid down by his great predecessor on the proportions of the body, the curve of the figure, the formation of a flowing silhouette, the graceful lines of the drapery. The "female type" with soft facial features framed by an abundance of hair also derives from Praxiteles. Tanagra figurines were made from well-worked clay, a pointed stick being used to mark the fine detail; then they were coated with a mixture of white clay, and painted with mineral pigments in vivid colors.

HELLENISTIC ART
Woman with a Lekythos
End of IV century B.C.
Terra-cotta; height 10¼″
From Tanagra (Boeotia)

ALEXANDRIAN ART. *The Gonzaga Cameo.*
This cameo is named after its first owners, the dukes of Gonzaga of Mantua. The artist gave an idealized appearance to the deified rulers of Egypt—Ptolemy Philadelphus and his wife Arsinoë.
The layers of the stone are used in a masterly way, to represent the hair, the helmet, the clothes. The upper layer is brown, the faces are engraved in the middle layer, which is milk-white with a bluish tinge; for Arsinoë's profile only a thin part of the stone is used, thanks to which additional nuances stand out and intensify the interplay between light and shade.

ITALIC GREEK ART. *Red-figure Amphora with Herakles Drunk.*   *p. 27*
Scenes of theatrical performances were often represented on vases of Ancient Italy. The composition of the painting on this vessel is clearly an evocation of the theatre. The main scene shows Herakles prostrate on the ground and a woman trying to revive him; but the crowd taking part in the event is represented in the background like the Chorus of a Classical Greek

ALEXANDRIAN ART
The Gonzaga Cameo
III century B.C.
Sardonyx; height 6⅛"
From Alexandria, Egypt

p. 27
ITALIC GREEK ART
Red-figure Amphora with Herakles Drunk
Sicily, last three decades of the IV century B.C.
Terra-cotta; height 12½"
Found in Sicily

tragedy during the action. Despite the limited range of the palette, the rhythm of the main patches of color succeeds in creating powerful effects.

SYRIA OR PHOENICIA. *Cantharus, or Deep Cup.*

The delicately chased mount, which reveals red glass in its upper part, is decorated with a frieze in deep relief representing hunters attacking wild boars, deer and other animals. The convex lower half of the cantharus is ornamented with garlands, shells, and volutes. The vessel was found in Mtskheta, Georgia.

COPTIC ART. *Medallion Representing the Earth Goddess Geb.*   *p. 29*

The bust of a young woman is woven in many-colored wool on the dark blue background of the medallion. The large Greek initial letters ΓΗ at the left signifying "earth" identify her as the Egyptian deity Geb. Her long hair, parted in the middle, falls in curls over her shoulders. She is wearing gold earrings in the form of the sacred Egyptian serpent, the *uraeus.* Her head is adorned with flowers, ears of wheat and a headband with the solar disc and again the *uraeus.* The goddess is wearing a tunic with a cloak thrown

SYRIA or PHOENICIA
Cantharus, or Deep Cup
III century A.D.
Glass, chased and engraved silver, gilt;
height 5¹¹/₁₆″
Found in Mtskheta, Georgia

COPTIC ART
Medallion Representing the Earth Goddess Geb
IV century A.D.
Flax, wool; tapestry weave; diameter 10″
Discovered at Akhmim, Egypt

over it, tied at the front with the so-called Isis knot. A horn of plenty can be seen in the folds of her cloak. The medallion is framed by a garland of flowers and leaves.

The rich and delicately harmonized color scheme of the fabric is made up of twelve different colored wools, all variously combined and shaded.

The medallion served as a shoulder ornament for a tunic. A twin medallion representing the Nile god is kept in the Pushkin State Museum, Moscow.

These medallions, discovered in a necropolis near Akhmim in the autumn of 1888, are magnificent specimens of early Coptic weaving.

BYZANTINE or ROMAN ART. *Bust of the Emperor Julian.*
This remarkable bust of the Emperor Julian is a magnificent piece of hard-stone carving from the transitional period between Roman and Byzantine art. The Emperor is represented wearing a cloak held by a fibula, and he has a bracelet on his right arm. The eyes were probably inlaid and there also was a metal diadem on the head.

This is a perfect example of the moment when the classical treatment of three-dimensional volume was combined with a new tendency towards surface, descriptive ornamentation, as seen here in the rendering of the beard, the hair and the drapery of the body.

Below
BYZANTINE or ROMAN ART
Bust of the Emperor Julian
IV century B.C.
Chalcedony; height 3⅜"

p. 31
BYZANTINE ART
Diptych Representing Gladiatorial Fights with Wild Beasts
V century A.D.
Carved ivory; height 13"; width of each leaf 4⅛"
From Constantinople

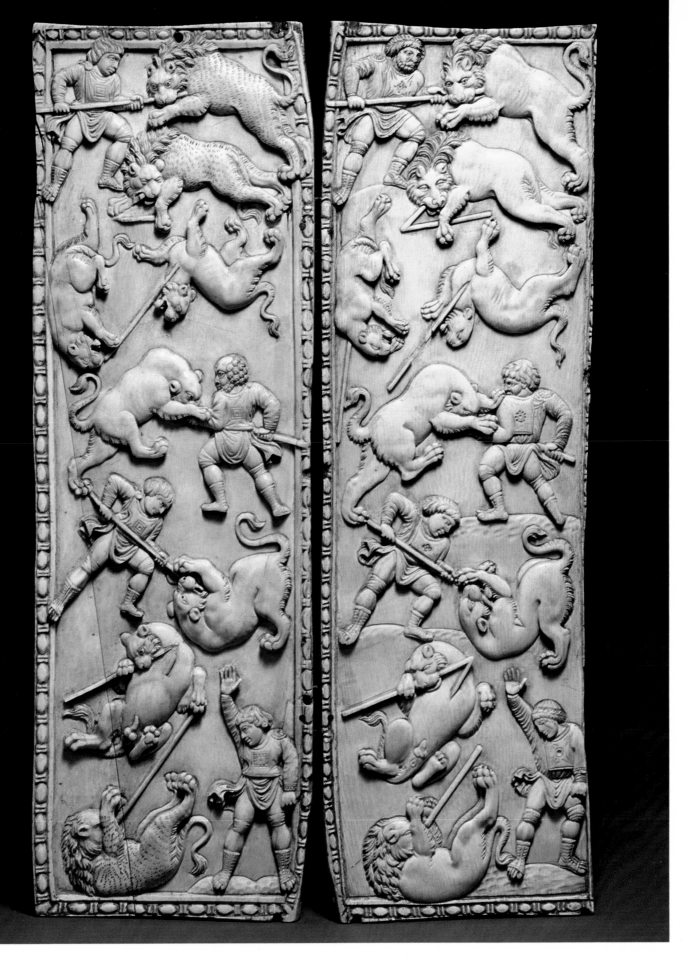

BYZANTINE ART. *Diptych Representing Gladiatorial Fights with Wild Beasts.*   *p. 31*

The most characteristic objects of ivory in early Byzantine art were the diptychs which were commissioned exclusively by newly appointed consuls. On assuming office, the consul would give performances for the people, which explains why circus or theatrical scenes are often represented.

On both leaves of this diptych are depicted gladiators in the circus, the so-called *venatores* (hunters), fighting lions and panthers. On their clothes can be seen individual symbols indicating that they belong to particular circus organizations. It is possible that the leaves were executed by two different craftsmen: on the right, the ground line is marked under each group, while on the left it is marked only under the lower one.

BYZANTINE ART
Triptych of the Forty Martyrs
First quarter of the XI century A.D.
Carved ivory; silver mount and coloring added
later; height 7¼"; width (when open) 9½"

BYZANTINE ART. *Triptych of the Forty Martyrs.*

In the center panel appears the scene of the Forty Soldier-Martyrs left to freeze to death on the Sebaste lake; above them is the figure of Christ in a nimbus, attended by angels. A Greek inscription is marked on the background. On the side panels stand soldier-saints in full length. At the top left are St. George and St. Theodore Tiron; below, Sts. Demetrius and Mercury. At the top right stand St. Eustace and St. Theodore Stratelates; and below, Sts. Eustrates and Procopius.

The triptych is notable for the high quality of the carving, the extraordinary expresssiveness in the individual characterization of the figures and the effectiveness of the composition. Nevertheless, some of the details—for example in the rendering of the leg muscles—seem to reflect the use of some model, and were perhaps based on paintings. On the shields of the soldier-saints Dimitri and Procope, and on the scabbard of Theodore Stratelates are inscriptions which imitate Arab writing. The color background and the silver mount were added later, perhaps in the Middle Ages.

On the exterior of the triptych when it is closed there is a four-armed cross with rosettes on the ends and one in the middle of the cross.

ARMENIAN ART. *Embossed Silver Bowl.*   *p. 34*

On a central medallion inside the bowl, the Biblical king David is represented together with the allegorical figure of Melody. The outside of the bowl is decorated with geometric and floral ornament, along with figures of horsemen, lions, sirens, griffins and birds. Elements of Byzantine, Islamic, Armenian and Western European art can all be identified in the shape and decoration of the bowl. The resemblance between the portrayal of the lions on the bowl and of lions on coins minted under the Cilician king Levone (end of the 12th to the beginning of the 13th century) enables us to define the place of manufacture of the vessel as being that of the Armenian kingdom of Cilicia, which had close links with Byzantium and with the Crusaders' states in Syria, as well as with Moslem principalities.

32   There is a similar bowl in the Kiev Museum of Western and Eastern Art.

ΟΙ ΑΓΙΟΙ ΤΕΟ ΔΡΑΚΟΝΤΑ

ARMENIAN ART. *Triptych-reliquary.*   *p. 35*

This triptych-reliquary was commissioned by Bishop Constantine, prior of the Skevra Monastery, as a memorial for the defenders of the Romkel fortress who were killed when it was destroyed by the Mamelukes in 1292. Although the reliquary has suffered considerable alterations, its artistic and historical significance remains very great. More than thirty Biblical characters are depicted on the inside of the triptych, as well as Gregory the Illuminator—apostle of Armenia—the national hero Vardan Mamikonian, and King Hethum II of Cilician Armenia.

The technical skill and great artistic sensitivity with which the figural and ornamental motives are executed, and the subtle correlation between the background, the figures and the inscriptions, place this reliquary among the greatest masterpieces of Armenian art.

In historical significance, the triptych reproduced here far surpasses all known works of Armenian silverwork—which are above all works of art. Few works of jeweled art in the world will be found to possess such a profound and complex concept developed with such incredible logic and expression as the Skevra reliquary. It has not only an abstract theological significance, but also a concrete, civic resonance. In it the tragic events of the history of Cilician Armenia of the end of the 13th century find their artistic reflection.

ARMENIAN ART
Triptych-reliquary
Skevra Monastery, Cilician Armenia, 1293
Wood, silver and gilt; height 25″

ARMENIAN ART
Embossed Silver Bowl
Cilician Armenia, late XII century
Silver and niello; diameter 10¼″

SYRIAN ART. *Horn.* p. 36

The shape of this horn, decorated with two bands of Arabic inscriptions and bearing the title of a ruler whose name is not mentioned, is unique. Between the two strips there are four figures of Christian saints. Syria's Christian population was fairly large in the Middle Ages (there have come down to us at least a dozen objects with Christian subjects which were made in Iraq and Syria in the 13th and 14th centuries).

The silver mount of the horn was made in 1551, possibly in Germany or in a Baltic country—it was commissioned by Bruno von Drolshagen, a member of the Order of the Livonian Knights.

IRANIAN ART. *Goblet.*

This thin-walled earthenware goblet decorated with feast scenes dates from the height of Persian ceramics when, along with traditional decorative techniques—such as relief and glazing—the application of luster and polychrome painting called *minai* began to be used. *Minai* is a type of fine-

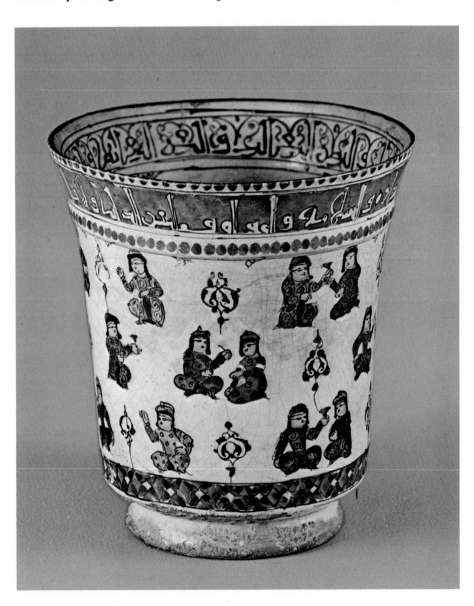

textured enamel in which the most delicate painting is fused into the surface of the vessel. Ceramics decorated in the *minai* technique preserve the purity of the colors, with muted tones which blend harmoniously.

Objects similar to the Hermitage goblet are generally associated with the production of the town of Rayy, preeminent as a center of ceramics in the 12th and 13th centuries.

IRANIAN ART. *Pitcher Representing the Winged Deity Senmurv and the Sacred Tree.*

In old Persian mythology, Senmurv, who is represented on this silver pitcher, was a fantastic creature generally depicted as having the head of a dog with his mouth open, the wings of a bird and a peacock's tail. His image appears on textiles, bas-reliefs, carpets and dishes. Senmurv was in fact a popular benevolent symbol and representations of this figure often decorated objects personally belonging to the king.

IRANIAN ART
Pitcher Representing the Winged Deity Senmurv
VI century A.D.
Silver, gold; height 13¼"

IRANIAN ART. *Dish Representing a Flying Goddess.*   *below*
The image on this dish is undoubtedly linked to an old Persian myth. It is
held by some to illustrate the myth, recorded in texts, of the goddess of fertility, Anahita, flying away on a fantastic bird. The scene might also symbolize the autumn equinox, an old Persian religious festival connected with
the period when flowering and fertility, personified by Anahita, leave the
Earth till the following spring.

IRANIAN ART. *Dish Representing the Shahinshah Shapur II
Hunting Lions.*   *p. 40*
Silver dishes representing Shahinshahs (Kings of Kings) at the time when
the Sassanid dynasty ruled Iran were considered precious gifts on which noblemen prided themselves.
The relative lack of detail in the portrayal on this dish is characteristic of
most works of Sassanid toreutics. The dish is executed in a technique of su-

IRANIAN ART
Dish Representing a Flying Goddess
IV century A.D.
Silver gilt; diameter 8⅝"

perimposed layers, with all the embossed elements chiseled separately then soldered together.

The back of the dish bears a Sogdian inscription which dates from the 7th–8th centuries and relates to the weight of the dish. Hence this article, which came out of the royal workshops of Shapur II (A.D. 309–379), turned up in Sogdiana three centuries after it was made and then, a century later, was taken to a locality not far from Perm in the Urals, where it was discovered in 1927 in a treasure trove.

IRANIAN ART
Dish Representing the Shahinshar Shapur II
Hunting Lions
IV century A.D.
Silver gilt; diameter 9¹/₁₆″
Discovered near Perm, in the Urals, 1927

ITALIAN ART

XIII—XVIII centuries

ART OF SOUTHERN ITALY. *Cameo of Joseph and his Brothers.*
The large dimensions of this carved stone, the many-figured composition, the perfection of the execution, as well as the Hebrew inscription have long attracted the attention of scholars; but both the dating and the provenance of the cameo have given rise to serious disagreement. Individual characters and whole groups in the cameo have definite parallels with the representations of the *Forty Martyrs* depicted in Byzantine mosaics and ivory plaques of the 10th and 11th centuries. But here, in contrast to its Byzantine prototypes, the figures have acquired volume, freedom of movement and the three-dimensional aspects of the composition as a whole remind one of proto-Renaissance Florentine plastic art. The question of the Venetian origin of the cameo has also arisen, since it is in the Venice of the 13th and 14th centuries that the Byzantine influence was at its strongest.
Today, it is customary to relate the Hermitage cameo and its simplified replica in the Royal Collection at Windsor to a group of objects of the Hohenstaufen period, or more specifically to the intaglio workshops which flourished under Frederick II Hohenstaufen, whose Sicilian court was a major center of culture in the Middle Ages.

ALESSANDRO MASNAGO. *Cameo of Apollo Slaying Python.*
The art of the Milanese gem-engraver Alessandro Masnago, who worked for many years on commission for Emperor Rudolph II, was a distinctive phenomenon of late Renaissance glyptic art. Instead of minerals with parallel stratifications of contrasting colors traditionally used for cameos, Masnago resorted to variegated agates or jasper, using their color distribution and veins to create miniature "pictorial compositions." In Paolo Morigia's celebrated book *La Nobilità di Milano,* published in 1595, the author describes Masnago's works: ". . . they are all made of variegated stones with many-colored blotches and veins which he is able to use, thanks to his remarkable talent, in such a way that they seem to be painted and colored." In addition to this, the carvings were always very deep, at times very close to high relief.
The cameo of *Apollo Slaying Python* is a magnificent example of Masnago's style. The yellow-white blotches on the dark grey background enabled the engraver to separate Apollo and the gods sitting on clouds, thereby giving an impression of light radiating from Jupiter and illuminating the place of the duel. The composition of the cameo is not original. As in many of his other works, Masnago borrowed the subject matter from the French engraver Etienne Delaune, who in turn reproduced in his engraving (in the series of *Apollo and Diana*) a drawing by Luca Penni. The Hermitage cameo thus offers a remarkable example of the reciprocal "transalpine" artistic influences, which enriched the countries north of the Alps as much as Italy itself.

PESELLINO (FRANCESCO DI STEFANO). *Allegory of Rome.*   *p. 44*
In the Hermitage collection there are six miniatures which formerly were part of the *Silius Italicus* codex. A seventh miniature still occupies its rightful place in the book, which is now in the San Marco Library in Venice. The codex was probably commissioned for the ordination of Pope Nicholas V, whose portrait appears on one of the pages now in the Hermitage. Gior-

ART OF SOUTHERN ITALY
Cameo with Joseph and his Brothers
Ca. 1240
Three-layered sardonyx;
$2\frac{1}{2}$" x $2^{15}/_{16}$" (with mount)
Inscription in Hebraic characters: "And as for you, go in peace unto your father." The cameo depicts one of the episodes of the Biblical story of Joseph, son of Jacob. Dressed like an Egyptian vice-ruler, holding a scepter in his hand, he is sitting on a throne before his brothers who had sold him into slavery in former days and now do not recognize him; he accuses the youngest one, Benjamin, of stealing a silver bowl which Joseph himself had ordered to be secretly put into Benjamin's bag. His brothers tear their clothes in despair and, stepping forward, Judah begs Joseph to let Benjamin go, and to make a slave of himself instead as a punishment.

ALESSANDRO MASNAGO
Cameo with Apollo Slaying Python
Milan, late XVI century
Agate; $1^{15}/_{16}$" x $2\frac{1}{4}$"

gio Vasari, describing these exquisite miniatures in great detail in his life of Fra Angelico, says that according to one Cosimo Bartoli, the artist who painted them was the miniaturist Attavante (1452—no later than 1517). However, these miniatures clearly belong to an earlier period, and show great affinity to the work of another Florentine artist Francesco di Stefano,

**PESELLINO
(FRANCESCO DI STEFANO)**
Florence ca. 1422—Florence 1457
Allegory of Rome
Gouache and gold on parchment;
11¼" x 8⅛"
(edges unevenly cut)

LEONARDO DA VINCI
Vinci 1452—Amboise 1519
Madonna with a Flower (Benois Madonna)
Oil on canvas, transferred from wood;
19½" x 12⅜"

44

45

called Pesellino, a younger contemporary and perhaps a pupil of Fra Filippo Lippi. Compare, for example, Pesellino's miniature *The Adoration of the Shepherds* (Louvre), or his painting *The Crucifixion* (Museum of Esztergom, Hungary), or *The Madonna and Child with Six Saints* (Metropolitan Museum, New York). It would appear that these pages from the *Silius Italicus* date from the later years of Pesellino's life, when he was at the height of his powers. The graceful figure of the young woman holding the scepter and the orb—the personification of victorious Rome—is delineated in light, elegant lines, against a background of sea and sky. The figure combines monumental grandeur with lively movement. The clear, pure colors, which have lost none of their original brightness, lend a particular splendor to the page.

LEONARDO DA VINCI. *Madonna with a Flower (Benois Madonna). p. 45*

The *Benois Madonna,* one of the few undisputed works by the master, dates from a relatively early period. We know this from a note by the artist on a sheet of sketches, which is now in the Uffizi Gallery, Florence, precisely dated 1478.

Leonardo painted religious subjects in the genre style which was so characteristic of the Italian Quattrocento. The young Mary, beautiful and calm, is holding out a flower toward her infant Son. The flower, with its four petals symbolizing the Crucifixion, is endowed with yet another, deeper significance in this picture, namely the enlightenment of the world, which began with the infant's first unsteady movements.

The delicate treatment of light and shade gives the figures a wonderful life-like quality. Leonardo's new, innovative style did not go unnoticed by his contemporaries. In a book entitled *The Treasures of Florence,* published in 1591, Bocchi wrote: "A small panel of remarkable beauty, painted by Leonardo da Vinci, in which the Madonna is depicted with great fascination and extraordinary mastery. The figure of the infant Christ is unusual, his raised face like no other and astonishing in the depth of meaning and successful execution."

ERCOLE DE ROBERTI. *Group Portrait of the Duke d'Este's Family.*

Ercole de Roberti was official painter in the court of the First Duke d'Este of Ferrara from 1486 on. This drawing is believed to show the Duke and his family in the following order: Ercole I (1431–1505) in the center; to the left his younger brother Sigismondo (1433–1507); on the right his eldest son and successor, Alfonso (1476–1534).

In fluent pen strokes, the artist models the figures with great mastery. By skillful construction of the scene and the low horizon, the noble figures attain impressive monumentality. Similar methods of composition and treatment of standing figures are also found in some of the artist's paintings, such as the *Procession to Golgotha* (Dresden Art Gallery), *The Israelites Gathering Manna* (National Gallery, London) and *The Miracles of St. Vincent Ferrer* (the Vatican Museum, Rome).

The drawing probably dates from around 1492. There is little to support the attempts that have been made to attribute the sheet in the Hermitage to Bernardo Parentino, whose style is somewhat coarser and more down to

ERCOLE DE' ROBERTI
Ferrara ca. 1456—Ferrara 1496
Group Portrait of the Duke d' Este's Family
Brown ink; 8¹/₁₆″ x 8¼″ (restorations in two upper corners).

pp. 48–49
MICHELANGELO BUONAROTTI
Caprese 1475—Rome 1564
Crouching Boy, ca. 1530–1534
Marble; height 21¼″

earth. There is a very similar, though slightly smaller drawing in the Victor de Stuers collection (Netherlands), which was shown in 1962 in an exhibition which went to Paris, Rotterdam and Haarlem, and was listed as an example of work from the school of Ferrara in the second half of the 15th century.

MICHELANGELO BUONARROTI. *Crouching Boy.* pp. 48–49

The sculpture of the *Crouching Boy* was acquired in 1787 as one of the works in the Lyde-Brown collection. It is said that it was once part of the Medici collection. The statue was in the Petersburg Academy of Arts until 1851 when it was transferred to the Hermitage.

One of the sketches for the Medici Chapel (now in the British Museum, London), shows two figures in niches, similar in pose to the *Crouching Boy,* viewed in profile. This leads to the assumption that the statue was originally intended to adorn the Medici Chapel. Some experts maintain that the *Crouching Boy* was given to one of Michelangelo's pupils to do—either to Pierino da Vinci or Tribolo. However, it is agreed by most that the high quality of the statue proves beyond a doubt that Michelangelo himself was responsible for it, though possibly with the help of assistants.

The symbolic meaning of the *Crouching Boy* is not quite clear. Some consider it the symbol of an unborn soul, others the spirit of death. The statue, however, manages to rise above all these suppositions—it is the tragic image of Man, bowed down by some evil force, suffering both physically and spiritually. On that level, the relationship of the *Crouching Boy* to other statues in the Medici Chapel can be clearly seen.

Most experts date *Crouching Boy* at about 1524, when work began on the Medici Chapel. However, stylistic analysis gives grounds to date the statue between 1530 and 1534, when Michelangelo, having already abandoned the idea of including it in the Chapel ensemble, could devote himself to it.

GIORGIONE. *Judith.* p. 51

Biblical subjects glorifying the heroic deeds of man, including the story of Judith, were frequent in Renaissance art. Giorgione's treatment of the theme is highly individual and unparalleled in the works of his contemporaries. The emphasis is not on the action but on the mental attitude of the heroine. In this painting Judith embodies the typical 16th-century ideal of beauty, not an abstract type of beauty, but one full of vital energy. Man and Nature are in perfect harmony, and this is the reason why rural scenery always plays such an important role in Giorgione's works. Giorgione, with his love of color, pays close attention to its effect on the surroundings in an effort to reproduce the play of light and air in an infinite variety of tones. Originally, the panel was used to decorate the door of a wall cupboard. Before its transfer onto canvas, it still had the marks of the hinges on the back, and during its restoration in 1967–1970, the place for the keyhole was discovered.

When it was in the Crozat Collection (with which it came to the Hermitage in 1772), *Judith* was attributed to Raphael. It is one of the few works of unquestioned attribution to Giorgione to have come down to us.

GIORGIONE
(GIORGIO DA CASTELFRANCO)
Castelfranco Veneto ca. 1478—Venice 1510
Judith
Oil on canvas, transferred from wood;
56⅝" x 26³⁄₁₆"

RAPHAEL (RAFFAELLO SANZIO). *Madonna and Child (Conestabile Madonna).*

RAPHAEL
(RAFFAELLO SANZIO)
Urbino 1483—Rome 1520
Madonna and Child (Conestabile Madonna)
Tempera on canvas, transferred from wood;
6⅛" x 7⅛"

The *Conestabile Madonna* is one of Raphael's earliest works, painted about 1502. The composition was suggested by a drawing by Raphael's teacher, Perugino, depicting the *Madonna and Child holding a Pomegranate.* In 1881, when the painting was transferred from wood to canvas, it was discovered that in the original version, Mary was holding a pomegranate out to the child. As he worked, the young artist changed his mind, without however modifying the final meaning of the painting in any way.

Countering the circular form of the tondo, which called for a deep understanding of composition, Raphael brilliantly resolved the problem. The

ANDREA DEL SARTO
(ANDREA VANUCCI)
Florence 1486—Florence 1530 or 1531
Madonna and Child with Sts. Catherine,
Elizabeth, and John the Baptist
Oil on canvas, transferred from wood;
40⅛" x 31½"
Signed below: *"Andrea del Sarto Florentino*
faciebat"

curve of the frame harmonizes with the gentle contours of the mantle covering the Madonna's head and shoulders. The traditional theme is treated simply and poetically. The spring landscape echoes the pure and feminine visage of the Madonna.

Before its transfer onto canvas, the wooden base and its gilded frame—no doubt also made by Raphael himself—were still all in one piece. The intricate, heavy carving of the frame beautifully sets off the delicate miniature painting.

The picture retains the typical Quattrocento tendency to narrative—details such as the boat crossing the lake, and the buildings on the shore are carefully done. Yet at the same time the crystal clarity of the forms and of the composition, and the beauty of line in this early work portend the future founder of the monumental style of the Roman school of painting.

ANDREA DEL SARTO. *Madonna with Child and Saints Catherine,*
Elizabeth and John the Baptist.
The artist has a new, direct approach to the traditional theme of "holy conversations," which is a continuation of the direction first introduced into the Florentine school by Leonardo da Vinci. The landscape background

CORREGGIO
(ANTONIO ALLEGRI)
Correggio ca. 1489—Correggio 1534
Portrait of a Lady
Oil on canvas; 40⁹/₁₆″ x 34⁷/₁₆″

against which Mary and the saints are depicted is unobtrusive, and leaves the attention concentrated on the group. The figures of the children, the infant Christ, laughingly throwing himself into his mother's arms, and the curly-headed, restless John, whom Elizabeth is lightly restraining, make the composition a very lively one.

This work is a superb example of High Renaissance art, with its strict conformity to the principle of being able to immediately identify the central subject, and its well-planned logic of movement. Leonardo da Vinci's influence can clearly be felt in the soft treatment of light and air. The beautiful harmony of colors shows that this problem interested Andrea del Sarto more than it did many other artists of the Florentine school.

CORREGGIO (ANTONIO ALLEGRI). *Portrait of a Woman.*

Correggio only very rarely produced portraits. This makes the portrait in the Hermitage even more interesting, with its complicated allegorical meaning. In the shade of a spreading laurel (obviously an allusion to the subject's poetic talents), sits a lady in a dark dress, holding a dish in her hand. The lady's full, somber-colored dress is either a sign that she is a member of some religious order, or that she is a widow. The trunk of the tree on the left is covered with ivy, symbol of eternity. On the inside of the dish is vis-

54

TITIAN
(TIZIANO VECELLIO)
Pieve di Cadore 1485–1490—
Venice 1576
St. Sebastian
Oil on canvas; 82⅝″ x 45¼″.
The painting remained in the
artist's studio until his death
and was not sold until 1581;
then the entire house and its
contents were sold by the
artist's son to Orazio Patrizio
Barbarigo. The picture
remained in the Barbarigo
Collection until 1845, when the
last surviving member of the
family died. Then a catalogue
was compiled and all the
pictures sold. In 1850 the
Hermitage bought five Titian
paintings, including the St.
Sebastian.

ible part of an inscription in Greek—it is from a line in Homer's *Odyssey,* describing how Helen puts a drug into the wine to chase sadness away. Some think that this is a portrait of Veronica Gamba, the poetess and wife of the ruler of the town of Correggio. It would seem that it was painted after the death of her husband, which occurred in 1518. The artist's signature has been deciphered, a name which had previously been assumed to be that of the lady herself or her lover. On the tree trunk is traced the name Anton Laet, which is the Latinized form of the artist's surname.

In the Hermitage portrait, Correggio reflects the new attitude toward women which was a product of the humanistic ideals of the Renaissance.

TITIAN (TIZIANO VECELLIO). *St. Sebastian.*   *p. 55*
Titian painted this picture in the final years of his life. The saint's face is illuminated by the smoky haze of a fire, which makes everything indistinct. It is almost as if the artist had carved the figure out of one great mass of color, with everything merging into a single tone. This particular treatment of form was so unusual that all his late works painted in this manner were believed by Titian's contemporaries to be unfinished.

Titian's original intention had been to paint a half-length image of St. Sebastian. In the process of his work he had to add a piece of canvas to the right side, and this piece was of a completely different texture. Then later on as the work progressed, Titian changed his mind and decided to paint a full-length figure. The top half of the painting is nearer completion than the bottom half, in which the sandals and the toes are only sketched in. It seems likely that Titian regarded this picture as a *"modello"* and therefore kept it in his studio. Later he painted another version, known to us today only from the testimony of Ridolfi (1648) and from a description of it by the Abbot Pons, who saw it in 1788 in the Escorial. Consequently the *St. Sebastian* is not the only version of this subject, as had been thought until recently.

BENVENUTO CELLINI (?) *Perseus.*
One of the most prominent personalities of the 16th century, Benvenuto Cellini was known to his contemporaries as a sculptor, jeweler, and medalist; but future generations could appreciate him also as a writer, the author of his own celebrated autobiography (written between 1558 and 1562, but not published until the 18th century).

The best, and best-known work of Cellini the sculptor is the bronze statue of Perseus, which was commissioned by the Duke Cosimo I de'Medici in 1545 and erected on the Loggia dei Lanzi in Florence on April 28, 1554. Perseus stands victor over the dead body of Medusa, holding her severed head in his left hand.

The bronze in the Hermitage gives an exact idea of the statue. But rather than being actually based on the monumental statue, it is more probably a replica of the bronze model by Cellini now in the National Museum of Florence. The superb craftsmanship of the Hermitage bronze also seems to confirm that it is itself the work of Cellini. However, its base decorated with the figures of Jupiter, Mercury, Athene and Danaë with the young Perseus, although an exact copy of the pedestal beneath the statue on the Loggia dei
Lanzi, was obviously made at a much later date.

BENVENUTO CELLINI (?)
Florence 1500—Florence 1571
Perseus, mid-XVI century
Bronze; height (with pedestal) 35⅞″; height of
figure alone 22⅝″

Pages 58–59
**TINTORETTO
(JACOPO ROBUSTI)**
Venice 1518—Venice 1594
Birth of John the Baptist
Oil on canvas; 71¼″ x 104¾″

TINTORETTO. *Birth of John the Baptist.*   *pp. 58–59*

In the 19th century this picture was called the *Birth of the Virgin Mary,* and people tried to identify it with the canvas mentioned by Carlo Ridolfi as one of the last works by the artist. However, judging by its style, the picture in the Hermitage belongs to an earlier period, probably the 1550s.

The picture is packed with vivid color. The figures are cleverly foreshortened. The artist painted the scene in the genre style and, through the many small domestic details, reproduced the atmosphere of a rich Venetian household.

It is known that in the 17th century, this picture became part of Cardinal Mazarin's collection in Paris.

Another version can be seen in the church of San Zaccaria in Venice.

PAOLO VERONESE
(PAOLO CALIARI)
Verona 1528—Venice 1588
Adoration of the Magi
Oil on canvas; 17¾" x 13⅝"

PAOLO VERONESE. *Adoration of the Magi.*   *p. 61*

Throughout his creative life, Veronese returned many times to the theme of the *Adoration of the Magi* which he visualized as a stirring, festive occasion. The version in the Hermitage is smaller than the others, yet this in no way detracts from the scope of the painting, which is so characteristic of works by this renowned Venetian master. The completeness of the picture, and the fact that it is executed on copper, would seem to disprove the theory that the *Adoration of the Magi* was conceived as a sketch for a larger work, specifically for a ceiling in the Venetian church of San Nicolò dei Frari. Despite the fact that the Madonna and Child are on the left side of the picture, the artist has made her the center of attention in the composition, by directing the movement of all the other figures toward her and through his use of color—Mary's cold blue dress immediately attracts the eye. The architectural background in the shape of elaborate ancient ruins, tall, straight Corinthian columns, feathery clouds in the sky, the greenery of the trees, forms an almost ceremonial backdrop for the foreground, which is full of the figures of people and animals. The camels and their driver in a white turban remind us that this is set in the Orient. It is said that the figure of Saint Joseph, in the act of lifting the transparent cloth covering the infant Jesus, is actually a self-portrait of Veronese.

CARAVAGGIO. *The Lute Player.*   *p. 62*

"He also made a painting of a youth playing a lute which was quite well drawn from nature; in it is a carafe of flowers filled with water in which one can easily distinguish the reflections of a window and other objects in the room. On the flowers is fresh dew which is rendered with exquisite accuracy. And this, he said, was the most beautiful painting he ever made." (Giovanni Baglione, translated by Walter Friedlaender, *Caravaggio Studies,* Princeton, New Jersey, 1955).

Although this is a picture of a youth singing to the accompaniment of a lute, it is not, like the artist's earlier works, a genre painting. Although it treats the same idea of love and harmony, linked with poetry, the approach is realistic. The youth, who was probably one of the young artist's friends, together with the objects surrounding him, are depicted just as the artist sees them, following his principle of art reflecting nature as if in a mirror.

60

Caravaggio was particularly fond of still life. In one of the music books is copied the beginning of a madrigal by Jacob Arcadelt which was popular at the beginning of the 16th century: *"Voi sapete ch'io v'amo"* (You know that I love you).

The Lute Player is probably the first work by the artist in which he makes full use of light and shade, a technique which was to become his specialty. Commissioned by Cardinal Francesco Maria del Monte—in whose house he was living at the time—the picture subsequently entered the Marquis Giustiniani's collection, where it remained until the collection was sold at a Paris auction in 1808. With the help of Vivant Denon, director of the Louvre, the picture was purchased at this auction for the Hermitage.

BARTOLOMEO SCHEDONI. *The Holy Family.*
This drawing was most probably a preparatory study for a painting. The figures and the wide, flowing robes of the Virgin are drawn in bold, expressive lines. Soft shading is employed to define volume and chiaroscuro. The

CARAVAGGIO
(MICHELANGELO MERISI)
Caravaggio 1573—Port 'Ercole 1610
The Lute Player
Oil on canvas; 37" x 46⅞"

BARTOLOMEO SCHEDONI
Formigine 1578—Parma 1615
Holy Family
Black chalk heightened with white on yellow
tinted paper; 12⁹/₁₆″ x 10⁹/₁₆″

treatment of form, the manner of the drawing, the technique and the combination of black and white chalk are all very characteristic traits of the drawings of Bartolomeo Schedoni, who was a painter and etcher at the turn of the 17th century. Unfortunately very few of his works have survived. The Hermitage sheet shows a clear similarity to other works of the artist, such as *Study of a Seated Woman* (Royal Collection, Windsor), and *Madonna and Child with Saints* (Ashmolean Museum, Oxford). The figure of Joseph in the Hermitage drawing, especially his hands, is very reminiscent of another sketch of the same saint, this one a preparatory sketch in oil, now in the Louvre, for the painting *St. Elizabeth Distributing Alms.* The sketch was executed in Parma, where the artist worked between 1607 and 1615, and is now in the Palazzo Reale in Naples. The Hermitage drawing would seem to belong to the same late period, when the artist was influenced by the work of Correggio and his contemporaries, the Carracci brothers, as can been seen in the particular interest in the play of light and his rejection of Mannerist forms.

GIAN LORENZO BERNINI
Naples 1598—Rome 1680
Self-Portrait, ca. 1675
Terra-cotta; height 18⅛"

GIAN LORENZO BERNINI. *Self Portrait.* p. 64

Bernini, a sculptor of extraordinary creativity and energy, produced many portraits during the course of his long life. Like his other works, they almost always carry the mark of Baroque theatricality. His subjects—popes, kings, cardinals, dukes, rich noblemen—bewilder the spectator with their magnificence. It is very rare to come across a portrait by Bernini of people close to him, not done by commission. The few that do exist show the artist's great skill in penetrating the subjects' inner world.

One of these works, which is probably all that remains of what was once a bust, is the head in the Hermitage. A comparison of this head with an engraving of Bernini, done by Giovanni Battista Gauli around 1675, leaves no doubt that this head is a portrait of the sculptor himself. The expressive modeling, the freedom and yet at the same time the depth of understanding with which the artist is portrayed, all point toward the fact that it was done by Bernini himself. The old master studied himself very critically and thoroughly. He made no attempt to leave out a single wrinkle or the fatigue in

GIAN LORENZO BERNINI
Naples 1598—Rome 1680
Ecstasy of St. Theresa, ca. 1645
Terra-cotta; height 10½"
This work, like most other Italian Baroque terracottas, became part of the famous Venetian collection of the Abbot Filippo Farsetti (1705–1774). The pride of this collection was the group of sketches and models by sculptors of the 17th to early 18th centuries. The Abbot's nephew, Antonio Francesco Farsetti, member of the Order of the Maltese Cross, gave the collection in 1800 to the Russian Czar Paul I, who a short time before had been elected Grand Master of the Order. The collection was first kept in the Academy of Arts Museum, and then in 1919 it was moved to the Hermitage.

his eyes, nor did he hide the bitter lines at the corners of his mouth. The main quality of the portrait, however, is the expressiveness of the face, which is full of energy and sharpness of mind—traits which, according to Bernini's contemporaries, were very characteristic of the artist.

GIAN LORENZO BERNINI. *The Ecstasy of St. Theresa.*   *p. 65*
One of Bernini's most important works, the marble group representing *The Ecstasy of St. Theresa,* on which he worked from 1645 to 1652, is the famous altarpiece in the Roman church of Santa Maria della Vittoria. The subject of the sculpture is the mystical vision of the Spanish nun, St. Theresa. She wrote: "I saw an angel next to me in flesh and blood. In his hand I saw a long arrow with a burning tip and it seemed that he plunged it several times into my heart. The pain was so terrible that I couldn't stop myself from crying out, but it was at the same time so sweet that I wanted it to last forever."
Bernini managed to portray these contradictory sentiments with incredible force. This first terra-cotta model differs somewhat from the finished work, but it has the same feeling of passion and the same virtuosity, which are so characteristic of Bernini's work.

GUERCINO (FRANCESCO BARBIERI DA CENTO).
The Apostle Peter Resurrecting Tabitha.   *p. 67*
This preparatory sketch served as a model for a painting of the same name by the artist, dated 1618 and now in the Pitti Gallery, Florence. However, there are significant changes in the painting, and even in the drawing itself there are alterations, so-called *"pentimenti,"* which indicate the complexity of the creative process and the artist's search for a more effective composition. The changes in the drawing are mostly in the position of the head of the woman kneeling over Tabitha's body.
Guercino was a leading draughtsman in the 17th century, a founder of the new style of drawing, whose influence was considerable.
Guercino employed a variety of techniques. He used pen-and-ink lines for detail, especially in landscape drawings, a free flowing style for sketches, and both pen and brush for drawings in which the contrast between the ink and the blank white paper almost creates the impression of color. This "pictorial" effect can be seen in the Hermitage drawing. The figures are drawn with free-flowing line; the washes define volume, emphasize the contrast between light and shade, creating the impression of sunshine and air.

GIUSEPPE MAZZUOLI THE ELDER. *The Death of Adonis.*   *p. 68*
This signed and dated marble group was made by the Sienese sculptor Giuseppe Mazzuoli, one of Bernini's followers. The artist chose a dramatic moment from ancient mythology—the death of Aphrodite's lover. Yet the treatment of this subject is far from dramatic. Adonis, depicted in an awkward movement, as though balancing on air, is trying to throw off a wild boar. His head is thrown back theatrically, and his face expresses suffering. Leaving aside the masterful composition and the remarkable attention to detail, it must be said that the figures are conventional and unoriginal. This is a very characteristic early 18th-century work, the main aim of which is purely and simply to be decorative and entertaining.

66

GUERCINO
(GIOVANNI FRANCESCO BARBIERI)
Cento 1591—Bologna 1666
The Apostle Peter Resurrecting Tabitha
Pen and wash, brown ink; 7⅞" x 9⁹⁄₁₆".
An engraving was made of this drawing, and included in the Klinger-Röttger publication of drawings in the Hermitage.

GIAMBATTISTA TIEPOLO. *Unidentified subject.* *p. 69*

The drawings of Giovanni Battista Tiepolo, the great 18th-century Venetian painter, decorator and sculptor, include some of the finest examples of his work. Many are connected to paintings either as studies for future compositions or for individual figures. But special interest attaches to his independent drawings, often having fantastic or allegorical subject matter.

The Hermitage sheet, drawn with delicately precise pen lines, is notable for its compactness of form and dynamic movement. The masterful brown wash, which creates the feeling of sun and air, filling the space and modeling the figures and objects, gives a peculiar vivacity to the group.

This drawing is stylistically related to Tiepolo's *Scherzi di fantasia* series of etchings, and dates from about 1750. As in other analogous drawings and etchings, the theme is not clear. The figures and objects have an allegorical 67

GIUSEPPE MAZZUOLI THE ELDER
Volterra (?) 1644—Rome 1725
The Death of Adonis, 1709
Marble; height 76″
Signed and dated: *"Joseph Mazzuoli a MDCCIX"*
This is one of Mazzuoli's best known works.
According to several sources, the artist worked
on it for thirty-one years. Originally intended as
a gift to the Danish king, the statue was sold
instead to Cardinal Barberini. The circumstances
under which it came to Russia are not known.

GIAMBATTISTA TIEPOLO
Venice 1696—Madrid 1770
Unidentified Subject, ca. 1750
Pen and brown wash; 11⁷/₁₆″ x 9¹³/₁₆″
This drawing is stylistically related to
Tiepolo's *Scherzi di fantasia* series of etchings.

meaning, which experts say has some connection with astrology and music. This type of drawing was intended for sale to collectors and connoisseurs.

CANALETTO. *Arrival of the French Ambassador in Venice.*
Views showing Venice, Rome and London, which Canaletto was the first to paint, were in great demand all over Europe. *The Arrival of the French Ambassador in Venice* and its sister picture *The Departure of the Venetian Doge from the Ceremony of the Blessing of the Adriatic Sea* (Pushkin Museum, Moscow) stand out as two of Canaletto's greatest works.
With his characteristic eye for topographical detail, Canaletto depicts the center of Venice with the Doge's Palace, the Piazzetta, the San Marco Library, the Church of Santa Maria della Salute. A master of composition, drawing, color, the artist depicts the very texture of the air, the horizon shrouded in damp mist, the sky stretching into infinity, the rippling water. With acute sensitivity he observed the transparent shadows cast by the clouds on the palace wall and reflections from the water penetrating the darkness beneath the arch of the bridge.
The canvas shows the ceremonial reception of the French Ambassador Jacques Vincent Languet, Comte de Jersey, on the 4th of November, 1726. Judging by its style, the picture was painted a little later.

CANALETTO
(GIOVANNI ANTONIO CANAL)
Venice 1697—Venice 1768
Arrival of the French Ambassador in Venice
Oil on canvas; 71¼" x 102⅛"

CARLO BARTOLOMEO RASTRELLI
Florence ca. 1675—Petersburg 1744
Portrait of Peter I, 1723–1729
Bronze; height 40⅛"
Signed bottom right: *"Cre Rastrelly
(Florentinvs) F."*

CARLO BARTOLOMEO RASTRELLI. *Portrait of Peter I.* *p. 71*

Carlo Bartolomeo Rastrelli belonged to the young generation of artists active during the Florentine Baroque period, the last flowering of the Florentine school. In 1716, already an established sculptor, he came to Russia where he remained for the rest of his days, becoming one of the founders of Russian New Era art. Most of Rastrelli's works are now in Moscow and Leningrad museums, and the monument he made to Peter I—the first equestrian statue to appear in Russia—now stands in one of Leningrad's squares.

A friend of Peter I, Rastrelli has left us a whole series of his portraits, the one in the Hermitage being among the best. He succeeded in creating a lively, expressive portrait of the Reformer-Czar. Obliged to work in bronze (there being no marble in Russia in those days), he nevertheless produced the richness of detail and the precision typical of marble, giving the feeling of fur, of lace, of armor. Every detail is important; for example, the relief he did on the left breastplate (depicting Peter carving a statue of a woman with a crown, scepter and orb) symbolizes the foundation of the New Russia by Czar Peter. In this way, by combining the pathos of Baroque with careful observation and allegory, Rastrelli created an expressive and meaningful portrait.

FRANCESCO GUARDI
Venice 1712—Venice 1793
Triumphal Gate on the Waterfront
Pen and brown wash, watercolor, opaque white;
11″ x 7½″

FRANCESCO GUARDI. *Triumphal Gate on the Waterfront.* *p. 73*

The bizarre arch of this gateway, beyond which a distant landscape stretches away out of view, is a recurrent motif in Guardi's work. The Hermitage possesses a painting with a similar subject and a drawing that is a variation on this theme. Guardi's arches are evidently inspired by some real structure that caught the artist's fancy, but they are not a representation of any actual edifice. They lack the visual accuracy which characterizes 18th-century *vedute*. It is more an architectural fantasy impregnated by a subtle poetic inclination which gives the artist free rein for creative experimentation.

The architecture seems to come to life in Guardi's drawing. The ivy-wreathed stone is warmed by the rays of the sun. The vapor rising from the lagoon fills the empty space. The shore, the sea, the buildings, the figures of the people—everything blends into an integral, complete vision of the city, the atmosphere and life which the artist seeks to capture.

The style of the drawing is very similar to all of Guardi's paintings—swift, broken lines, oddly curving here and there, create the impression of movement, of a quivering atmosphere around everything. The contrast between sunlight and deep shade is rendered by brown washes of varying intensity. The watercolor of the sky appears to have been added by another artist.

JEAN-JACQUES CAFFIERI. *Portrait of the Comtesse du Barry.* *p. 74*

Marie Jeanne Bécu, Comtesse du Barry (1746–1793), patron of many artists and favorite of King Louis XV, was found guilty during the French Revolution of helping émigré aristocrats and was sent to the guillotine in 1793. Caffieri portrays Madame du Barry at the height of her beauty and fame, her head held haughtily high. Her lace-trimmed blouse, the garlands of

roses cleverly adorning the outline of her bust, her intricate hairstyle, everything gives this portrait an unusual feeling of elegance and lightness, while at the same time the rather indifferent modeling of the neck, shoulders and face with its shallow features is not particularly expressive.

At that period it was common in both painting and sculpture to depict the subject of a portrait in the guise of a Greek god or in theatrical costume. In this portrait Comtesse du Barry appears to be wearing a costume for a theatrical performance at court. The idealization, the embellishments, the technical virtuosity, accompanied by superficial characterization, are all typical of French aristocratic portraiture of the middle of the 18th century.

JEAN-JACQUES CAFFIERI
Paris 1725—Paris 1792
Portrait of the Comtesse du Barry
Marble; height 26⅛"

74

FLEMISH, DUTCH ART

XV—XIX centuries

ROGIER VAN DER WEYDEN. *Saint Luke Drawing the Virgin.*
The subject of this painting is the apocryphal legend about the Apostle Luke drawing a miraculous portrait of the Virgin when she appeared to him in a vision. In the 14th and 15th centuries, St. Luke was considered the patron saint of artists, and numerous painters' studios and guilds were named after him. It is an established fact that Rogier van der Weyden painted an altarpiece called *St. Luke Drawing the Virgin* for the chapel of the painters' guild in Brussels. The picture was very popular in the 15th century, and many versions were produced, the best of which are now to be found in the Boston Museum, in Bruges, in Munich, and in Leningrad. The Boston picture is considered by many to be the original; however it seems highly probable that they are all copies, albeit good ones, and that the original has not come down to us.

St. Luke is depicted in early 15th-century costume, and it could well be that his figure is actually a portrait of van der Weyden himself. He has wonderfully captured the inspiration of the artist at work. Rogier van der Weyden, like most Netherlandish artists, worked in oils, using the techniques first introduced by van Eyck. He uses bright colors to reproduce the richness of the materials and the golden embroidery. Precious stones gleam around the hem of the Virgin's dress—rubies and sapphires, casting little aureoles of red and blue light.

In the background, beyond the turreted wall of the hanging garden, a vast landscape sweeps off into the distance. The river winds its way, lapping at sandy banks. On rising ground lies a large town crammed with tiny houses, winding streets, and numerous people moving around, providing a view of the daily life of a medieval town.

In the 19th century, the upper part of this painting, showing the capitals of the columns and the wall above, was lost.

ROGIER VAN DER WEYDEN
Tournai 1399—Brussels 1464
St. Luke Drawing the Virgin
Oil on canvas, transferred from wood;
40⅛" x 42¼"

HENDRIK GOLTZIUS. *Mary Magdalene.*   *p. 78*
In addition to the figural compositions and landscape drawings of Goltzius there are quite a number of portraits, the earliest of which date from around 1570. Sometimes they were preparatory sketches for engravings, but more often they were complete works in their own right.

This drawing seems to be related to a late group of feminine portraits. The same manner is found in the works of Goltzius' young followers, such as the Dutch graphic artists Jacob Matham and Jan Muller.

The technique of "three crayons" (black chalk, sanguine, and white chalk) employed by the artist in his work was borrowed from Italy. Together with Rubens, Goltzius was one of the exponents of "three crayon" draughtmanship in the Netherlands. But in contrast to Rubens, Goltzius' style remained strictly graphic, never seeking the soft, painterly effects achieved by Rubens.

FRANS HALS. *Young Man with a Glove in his Hand.*   *p. 79*
Frans Hals was first and foremost a portrait painter. The portraits he created of his contemporaries are representative of a generation which secured decisive victories in the attempt to free itself from feudalism, and developed a vigorous and fruitful activity in the economic, political, scientific and artistic life of 17th-century Holland. The series of group portraits of corpo-

rations he painted were the greatest of his time. No artist before him succeeded in depicting with such depth the spirit of democratic solidarity and the faith in the common cause which aroused the contemporary Dutch society.

In portraits like the *Young Man with a Glove in his Hand,* Hals carefully preserves the characteristic traits and individuality of the sitter, yet manages at the same time to emphasize the inherent features which were typical of the Dutch of the first post-revolutionary decade, namely the heightened rhythm of life and optimistic attitude. The sharp foreshortening of the pose and the movement of the hands convey a momentary impression. Hals's

HENDRIK GOLTZIUS
Mühlbracht 1558—Haarlem 1617
Mary Magdalene
Black chalk, sanguine, heightened with white on
gray paper; 9⁷/₁₆″ x 7½″
Signed with monogram and dated: *"HG 1606"*

unique painterly manner—broad, free and sweeping—matches the dynamism of the picture. The tonal unity of the color emphasizes the integral
impression of the image.

The station in life of the young man portrayed in the Hermitage picture is
not clearly established, inasmuch as Hals made no attempt to indicate his
profession by any definite attributes, but some indirect intimations enable
us to assume that he is a doctor.

PIETER PAUL RUBENS. *Landscape with a Dam.*   *p. 80*

This drawing, one of Rubens' best, is an evocation of some place between
Vilvoorte and Mechelen where he worked during the last years of his life.
In this work Rubens created a profoundly lyrical and poetic image of nature. But the drawing is not taken from life, as indicated by the large dimensions of the sheet, the complicated technique, the studied composition

FRANS HALS
Antwerp 1581/1585—Haarlem 1666
Young Man with a Glove in his Hand, ca. 1640
Oil on canvas; 31½″ x 27″
Signed on background: *"FH"*

and absence of extraneous detail. The sheet might possibly have served as a design for a painting, if indeed it was not actually intended as a complete work of art in the fullest sense.

Not all experts agree on the attribution of this *Landscape with a Dam* to Rubens. Part of the reason for this is that the drawing differs from his known landscape studies in that it is not done directly from nature, but was drawn in his studio, and therefore is not a "portrait" of a particular place, but rather a general impression of it.

PIETER PAUL RUBENS. *Landscape with a Rainbow.*   *p. 81*

In the 1630s Rubens' landscape painting was at its height of perfection. *Landscape with a Rainbow* in the Hermitage, painted between 1632 and 1635, is one of the most notable works of the artist from that period. Rubens has chosen a rare moment in nature. A storm has just blown over and in the distance, caught in the rays of the sun, the heavens are illumined by an enormous rainbow, which seems to enclose the buildings and the landscape in the background. In the foreground is seen a rural idyll—young lovers listen to a shepherd playing a pipe while sheep graze peacefully around

80

PIETER PAUL RUBENS
Sieghen 1577—Antwerp 1640
Landscape with a Dam, ca. 1635
Gouache, tempera, black chalk, on paper (the upper corners cut off) 17⅛″ x 23¼″
The critic Jacob Burckhardt and others compare the Hermitage sheet with *Carriage Crossing a Stream,* a large drawing in black and white chalk on paper (National Gallery, London), in which the motif of the Hermitage drawing is developed and expanded.

them. The *Landscape with a Rainbow* could be considered the rural counterpart to Rubens' gallant picture of *The Garden of Love* (Prado Museum, Madrid, and the Rothschild Collection, England), with just one difference; in one case the characters are beautifully dressed cavaliers and ladies, while in the other they are shepherds and shepherdesses.

Landscape with a Rainbow differs from Rubens' landscapes of the preceding decade, which were typically charged with electric vitality. Here, the painting is enveloped in a spirit of harmony, a well-balanced composition following the basic rules of design, reflecting Rubens' study of the classical works of the Italian Renaissance, in particular of the Venetians, especially Titian. In the works of these masters can be traced prototypes of the overall composition and individual motifs in this canvas. However, the heightened luminous effects, the intermittent patches of light and shade, the dynamic color lend a tension to the picture that is not found in the classical works of the Renaissance.

PIETER PAUL RUBENS
Sieghen 1577—Antwerp 1640
Landscape with a Rainbow, 1632–1635
Oil on canvas, transferred from wood;
33⅞″ x 51³/₁₆″

81

ROELANT SAVERY. *The Country Fair (Peasant Holiday).*

This is one of the artist's most important drawings, executed during his first years in Prague at the court of Rudolph II. The high viewpoint, the varied activity in this scene of ordinary life, and the true democratic spirit of the old Netherlandish traditions, are all elements which descend from the work of Pieter Breughel the Elder.

This particular drawing, dated and signed by Savery, has particular significance today in connection with the question concerning the author of a famous series of drawings *naer het leven* (i.e., drawn from life), traditionally attributed to Pieter Breughel the Elder. The two horses in harness depicted in the Hermitage drawing, which are exactly the same as in a study in the Albertina, Vienna (inv. No. 7867), and several figures in the foreground are vital elements supporting the definitive attribution of the series now to Roelant Savery.

Unfortunately very few such large drawings, executed as was then called "in color with water," have come down to us. The reason for this is that this particular medium does not stand up well to the ravages of time and atmosphere. This makes the few examples which are found in the collections of major museums today all the more valuable.

ROELANT SAVERY
Courtrai 1576—Utrecht 1639
The Country Fair (Peasant Holiday)
Watercolor and gouache over black chalk, gold;
18⅞″ x 29¼″
Signed and dated bottom center: *"Roeland Savery fec 1606"*

ANTHONY VAN DYCK. *Portrait of Anna Dalkeith, Countess of Morton (?) and Anna Kirk.*   *pp. 84-85*

This portrait of two ladies-in-waiting of the English queen, Henrietta-Maria, is one of the later works of van Dyck (painted toward the end of the 1630s). This type of formal portrait brought fame to the artist in the highest circles of English society, whose favorite he became. On the eve of the English bourgeois revolution, van Dyck created the ideal of elegance and refinement which set the short-sighted and conceited English aristocracy apart from the bourgeoisie, whose roots lay in the people, their enemies and future vanquishers.

Both ladies have empty, doll-like faces and identical mannerisms. Both have long, extremely elegant figures, small heads, calm, beautifully made-up faces. However, they do differ. The elder has a slight, complacent smile on her face, while the younger has an air of cool detachment. The snobbishness of the aristocracy, their feeling of superiority over the crowd is emphasized by their rich, exquisitely beautiful clothes, rendered with all the splendor

Pp. 84–85

ANTHONY VAN DYCK
Antwerp 1599—London 1641
*Portrait of Anna Dalkeith, Countess of Morton(?)
and Anna Kirk,* ca. 1640
Oil on canvas; 51⁹⁄₁₆″ x 59¼″

of van Dyck's masterful execution. The shining silk dresses, silver-white and pale lilac, cherry-red and dark gray, harmonize with their tender, rosy complexions and gleaming ringlets and pearls. The artist's stroke is light, fleeting, transparent. The painting is full of rich layers of colors and contrasting tones.

The landscape background is superb. Romantic, emotional and spiritual—it recalls the landscapes of van Dyck's teacher, Rubens.

JACOB JORDAENS. *The Bean King.*
Jordaens repeated and varied this theme of the national holiday celebrating "the Three Kings" many times. Versions of *The Bean King* are to be found in the Gallery of Fine Arts, Brussels, the Cassell Picture Gallery, the Valenciennes Art Gallery, and the Louvre in Paris. These works made him famous. The title of the picture is taken from the tradition of annually crowning a carnival king on the sixth of January. Everybody is given a piece of pie, and the person who finds the bean baked into his slice is made the king. Jordaens' somewhat unusual, rather down-to-earth scene captures the atmosphere beautifully. The feeling that it is good to be alive pervades this picture of revelry. The crowding in of huge bodies seems almost to strain the limits of the frame and gives the impression of movement and disorder. One can almost hear the songs and shouts of the noisy revelers, and the technique of half-length portraiture which Jordaens learned from Caravaggio seems to bring one physically close to the characters. The bright colors built up in warm tones, the dynamic excitement of the carousing figures give the domestic scene the air of being an event of some importance. Jordaens, a true Flemish artist, still under the influence of Rubens' technique in many respects, creates a special type of genre picture, which differs from the "cheerful company" of the followers of Caravaggio and also from the Dutch tavern scenes.

JACOB JORDAENS
Antwerp 1593—Antwerp 1678
The Bean King, ca. 1638
Oil on canvas; 63″ x 83⅞″

REMBRANDT VAN RIJN. *Descent from the Cross.* *p. 89*

REMBRANDT VAN RIJN
Leyden 1606—Amsterdam 1669
Descent from the Cross
Oil on canvas; 62¼" x 46"
Signed and dated, bottom center:
"Rembrandt f. 1634"

Rembrandt's depiction of the tragic gospel story is amazingly lifelike. Christ's death has plunged the characters into profound agony. Mary, his mother, has lost consciousness, the women are sobbing, the men suffer in silence. The face of Joseph of Arimathea, one of Christ's most faithful disciples, is particularly expressive—in it we read a mixture of physical tension and spiritual torment. The action takes place at night by torch and candlelight. Three sources of light, each of differing strength, break through the darkness to illuminate the three main groups. Rembrandt's use of light to draw together and unite a composition of many different figures, together with his depiction of each individual character's feelings are his supreme achievement.

The picture in the Hermitage was Rembrandt's second on this theme. The first version, dated 1633, now in the Pinakothek, Munich, was part of the series of *Passions* painted for the Stadholder of the Netherlands. The picture was favorably received by its high-ranking purchaser; but it seems that the artist was not satisfied with his work, for a year later he painted another, the version which now hangs in the Hermitage. This one was more successful—at least Rembrandt thought so—and it remained in his house until 1656. In it Rembrandt managed to express that "elevated and truly natural flow of movement" which he talks about in one of his letters and by which he means not so much exterior expression as that of the inner soul.

REMBRANDT VAN RIJN. *Landscape with a Horseman.* *p. 90*

This landscape is obviously invented by Rembrandt, although it may reflect the reminiscence of a real landscape he had seen. Exactly the same church steeple, for instance, appears in his drawing *Small Bridge over a Canal,* now in the Teylers Museum, Haarlem. The "composed" effect is heightened by the carefully positioned stylish horseman and his servant (originally the boy-servant had been positioned further over to the right, but the artist deleted that figure).

The clump of trees in the center of the middle distance, as noted by O. Benesch, is similar to the trees in *Farm next to a Roadside,* now in the Oxford Museum. The dead tree on the knoll behind the horseman closely resembles the tree at the left in the above-mentioned *Small Bridge over a Canal.*

The placing of the figures of the horseman and the boy-servant closer together, which at first might seem insignificant, greatly increases the impression of the group's movement. In the original position, the boy-servant was rather "left out" of the group.

REMBRANDT VAN RIJN. *Flora.*   *p. 91*

The year he married Saskia van Uylenbruck (1634) Rembrandt portrayed her as Flora, the goddess of flowers. His manner of depicting drapery and embroidery on exotic materials, as well as petals of flowers, echoes that of his teacher, Pieter Lastman. But Rembrandt's cloth has consistency and weight, and the flowers are live and substantial. The contours of Saskia's figure slowly emerge from the somber background. The colors in the picture are a finely attuned harmony of gray-greens and golden tones.

It is said that in the 1630s Rembrandt did not pay much attention to the psychology of his models or to their inner, spiritual life. In the Hermitage picture Saskia is young, a girl still, seemingly self-conscious in her finery, with the heavy garland making her head lean forward a little, and timidly holding the flowery staff and the folds of her elegant cape in her hands. A year later Rembrandt was once again to paint Saskia's portrait as Flora (National Gallery, London)—and the change in the model is astonishing. Saskia-Flora in the London picture has become only one year older, but in that year she has blossomed out into a confident young woman who effortlessly portrays the role of a goddess—her head is held proudly high, her shoulders are straight and her face has an expression of decisiveness.

REMBRANDT VAN RIJN
Leyden 1606—Amsterdam 1678
Landscape with Horseman, between 1648 and 1650
Pen and wash, brown ink, with opaque white (the violet washes possibly added later, in another hand)

REMBRANDT VAN RIJN
Leyden 1606—Amsterdam 1669
Flora
Oil on canvas; 49¼″ x 39¼″
Signed and dated lower left:
"Rembrandt f. 1634"

JAN FYT. *Dogs Falling on a Fox.*
This colored sketch, one of the Flemish master's outstanding and best preserved drawings, is the model for a painting which has not survived. The
perfect knowledge of the animals' anatomy and behavior, and the high pictorial and decorative quality of the drawing—characteristics which distinguish Fyt's work—are the result of accumulated experience of many
generations of Flemish artists and their continual study of nature. Almost
every one of Fyt's paintings was preceded by numerous studies from life.
The studies for this drawing are to be found in the Hermitage and in the
Antwerp Print Room. Despite the traditional attribution of this drawing to
Jan Fyt, an attribution which goes back to the early 18th century, it came
to be considered in the late 19th and early 20th century as the work of the
French painter Jean-Baptiste Oudry. But it is precisely works like these
which show how much Oudry was indebted to his Flemish predecessor.

JAN FYT
Antwerp 1611—Antwerp 1661
Dogs Falling on a Fox
Gouache over black crayon, on yellow-gray
paper; 20″ x 20⅜″

GERARD TERBORCH
Zwolle 1617—Deventer 1681
A Glass of Lemonade, 1663–1664
Oil on canvas; transferred from wood;
26⅜" x 21¼"

GERARD TERBORCH. *A Glass of Lemonade.*
In the works of Terborch Dutch genre painting reaches its classic expression. His bare interiors, sparsely peopled by subjects who always blend in with their surroundings, became the model both for his contemporaries and for subsequent generations of artists. Terborch and other artists in his circle defined the course of Dutch art throughout the second half of the 17th century. Their art doubtlessly reflects the changes in the tenor of life and the tastes of the aristocratic Dutch elite. In place of the creative violence of Frans Hals' dynamic, sparkling canvases came delicate refinement, and boldness gave way to measure and discretion.
A Glass of Lemonade is one of Terborch's best and most famous works, and is a real masterpiece of Dutch painting. The artist's mastery—his superb draughtsmanship and feeling for the finest shades of color is manifest in his portrayal not only of silk and velvet, but also of glass and metal, fur and wood. With the same inimitable style he uncovers the inner, intimate world of his characters. Not until Terborch did genre painting become capable of expressing the most complex, barely perceptible human emotions.

93

JACOB VAN RUYSDAEL. *Landscape with a Stone Bridge.*

This study from nature, done in black crayon, with a gray wash added per-haps later in the studio, dates from about 1647, judging from its resem-blance to an etching of that date. The short, abrupt strokes (especially the foilage of the old oak) are very reminiscent of the technique of Ruysdael's teacher, Cornelius Vroom, which would also support the theory of its being an early work. The realism with which Ruysdael depicts the native land-scape rests on a rigorous observation of nature. But subsequently, in the in-terest of greater expression and creating a "landscape mood," this realism was somewhat elaborated in the studio. The artist would then make even greater departures from his realistic studies in the final painting. The Rijks-museum of Amsterdam now possesses Ruysdael's painting *Landscape with a Stone Bridge,* dated 1647, wherein the motif has been further altered.

PIETER DE HOOCH. *The Lady and the Maidservant.* *p. 95*

Pieter de Hooch was an outstanding Dutch genre artist whose favorite sub-ject was the unhurried way of life of the comfortable bourgeois, shut away in his own little world, surrounded by the four walls of his house, where the troubles and worries of the real world outside could not reach him. The town of Delft, where *The Lady and the Maidservant* was painted, was still

JACOB VAN RUYSDAEL
Haarlem 1628—Haarlem 1682
Landscape with a Stone Bridge, ca. 1647
Black chalk and gray wash; 6½" x 8⅛"
Among the works closest to the Hermitage
drawing may be cited the *Peasant Hut on the
River Bank* from the Luchta collection in Paris,
and *Hunter with Dogs in a Forest Glade* in the
Kupferstichkabinett, Berlin.

PIETER DE HOOCH
Rotterdam 1629—Amsterdam, after 1684
The Lady and the Maidservant
Oil on canvas; 20⅞″ x 16½″

in the 17th century a quiet, untroubled place. The bright golden light that the picture is bathed in reinforces the impression of an ordered way of life and gives the scene an air of placidity and blissful comfort.

The Hermitage painting belongs to the period when the artist was blossoming into full maturity. In those years he painted in beautiful blues, yellows and reds, producing paintings which are fascinating for their perfectly structured alternation of dark and light rooms, staircases, passages and arches, through which we can get a peep at a canal, or a row of houses on the other side of the street. Pieter de Hooch's interiors are always warmed by the presence of people and the poetry of their day-to-day life.

After 1660 the artist left Delft and went to Amsterdam where his work underwent a considerable change and began to decline.

VINCENT VAN GOGH. *Memory of the Garden at Etten (Ladies of Arles).*

p. 96

In this picture—painted in 1888 when van Gogh and Gauguin were living together at Arles—van Gogh borrowed Gauguin's motif in *Ladies of the Garden* (Chicago Art Institute) of a winding, narrow road as a background to his painting of two Arles ladies, who appear in the lower left-hand side of the composition. Nevertheless, the pictures, despite their common ele-

ments, are very different. While the path in Gauguin's picture cuts past a gate in the foreground in a straight line between small pyramid-shaped bushes, van Gogh's path leading from the Arles Hospital is like a tumultuous river, and his cypresses like tongues of fire. The traditional distinction between figures and background disappears in this picture, where everything merges in the same restless rhythm, and behind the "flaming gothic" in which there is a tension of violent emotion pushed to the extreme. As if to counteract Gauguin's evenly applied color, van Gogh gives an excessive texture to his paint surface, loading the canvas to the point where it has become one of the most difficult works to preserve.

Memory of the Garden at Etten also reflects the impressions left on van Gogh by Seurat's and Signac's pictures. However, this work, rather than confirming their technique of juxtaposing small dots of contrasting and complementary colors, actually refutes the canons of Neo-Impressionism, inasmuch as van Gogh does not use it for optical mixtures, but rather to energize the color to an extreme degree.

VINCENT VAN GOGH
Groot Zundert 1853—Auvers-sur-Oise 1890
Memory of the Garden at Etten (Ladies of Arles), 1888
Oil on canvas; 29⅛" x 36⁹⁄₁₆"
This canvas, which the artist kept for his bedroom, was not painted from life but was inspired by memories of the Arles hospital garden, as well as his parents' garden in his home town of Etten.

96

FRENCH ART

XIII—XX centuries

JEAN DE CAMBRAI. *A Mourner.*   *p. 99, l.*

Still too little is known about 15th-century Netherlandish sculpture and its relationships with French art. Our knowledge about it is nothing compared to what we know of Netherlandish painting of the same period. The same experimentation was going on in sculpture as in painting, the proof of which are the few characteristic pieces in the Hermitage, which enable us to get some idea of Netherlandish sculpture of the time.

The statuette of *A Mourner* comes from the tomb of the Duke Jean de Berry (died 1416) in Bruges. Work on the tomb was started while the Duke was still alive, and was continued until the middle of the 15th century, with several different masters participating. Following the destruction of the tomb in 1757, the figurines of the mourners were dispersed.

This statuette of *A Mourner* dates from the early period of work on the tomb and is attributed to the artist Jean de Cambrai. Clearly influenced by Klaus Sluter, a leading Netherlandish sculptor at the turn of the 15th century, the work already gives signs of the new ideas and trends springing up.

ÉTIENNE BOBILLET and **PAUL MOSSELMAN.** *A Mourner.*   *p. 99, r.*

This statuette also comes from the tomb of Duke Jean de Berry in Bruges, but is of a later period than the preceding example, dating from approximately the middle of the 15th century. The works of Bobillet and Mosselman are characterized by a sensitivity of emotion and vehement expression—sometimes even going as far as exaltation—traits which are typical of 15th-century Netherlandish art.

The figure of this mourner, his robe hanging in well defined, strong folds, is very expressive. The hands are crossed on the breast in a gesture of resignation. The face is almost entirely hidden by the hood, but the very bowing of the head indicates great sorrow.

Comparing the statue with contemporary paintings, one is immediately reminded of the expressive, exalted art of Rogier van der Weyden. Nobody before Rogier could achieve such complete visual expression of different levels of human emotion from quiet sadness to utter despair.

FRENCH ART. *Portrait of Charles VII.*   *p. 100*

This portrait of Charles VII attracts attention first of all by the peculiarity of its treatment—it is executed in a special technique which combines carved semiprecious stones with faceted precious stones, gold, and enamel. This method originated in the 15th century but extremely few examples have survived from that period.

The face and neck are carved in milky-white chalcedony, the crown in garnets, and the collar is adorned with an emerald (perhaps mounted at a later date), and with enamel on gold; enamel also covers the gold garland of fine stylized leaves which surrounds the head. All the different parts are laid over gold plates and fastened together with thin mounts; but the background, which is usual in a cameo, is absent. The openwork, the beauty of the object and its brilliant decorative elements are combined with the masterful quality of the carving which evokes the singularity of the personage portrayed and deepens the psychological characterization. All this makes the cameo a magnificient example of the art of gem carving, jewelry and enameling in France at its culmination toward the end of the 14th century and the beginning of the 15th.

98

p. 99, left
JEAN DE CAMBRAI
? ca. 1355—Bourges 1438
A Mourner, before 1416
Marble; height 16⅞⁄₁₆″

p. 99, right
ÉTIENNE BOBILLET and PAUL MUSSELMAN
Active in the middle of the XV century
A Mourner, between 1450 and ca. 1456
Marble; height 16¼″

FRENCH ART. *Reliquary in the Form of a Deacon.*   *below right*
In this masterpiece of French jewel-work the character of Romanesque art becomes strikingly apparent in the solemnity and monumentality of the figure—in the unity of its mass. The artist avoids superfluous, trivial details: the elegant outline, the vertical folds of the dress, the abundance of smooth, shiny surfaces, all contribute to an impression of sublimity.

The reliquary probably represents St. Stephen, a deacon of the early Christian community who, according to the *Acts of the Apostles,* was stoned to death at the time of Christian persecutions. One can regard the stones which adorn the reliquary as attributes of his martyrdom.

The saint's relic was kept in the book which the deacon is holding.

JEAN FOUQUET. *Portrait of a Man.*   *p. 101*
The Hermitage possesses over a hundred and twenty crayon drawings of

Below left
FRENCH ART
Portrait of Charles VII
Ca. 1420–1429
Chalcedony, garnet, emerald, gold, enamel; 1³⁄₁₆″ x 1¹⁄₁₆″ (including the mount)
The portrait dates from the 1420s and seems to antedate the famous portraits of Charles VII— the picturesque portrait attributed to Fouquet, in the Louvre, dates from the beginning of the 1440s; the medal, from 1541; and the posthumous bust on his tomb, from 1463. This cameo significantly enriches the iconography of the French King.

Below right
FRENCH ART–END OF XII CENTURY
Reliquary in the Form of a Deacon
Silver, precious stones, glass, wood; hammered on wooden base, chased, filigreed; height 16½″

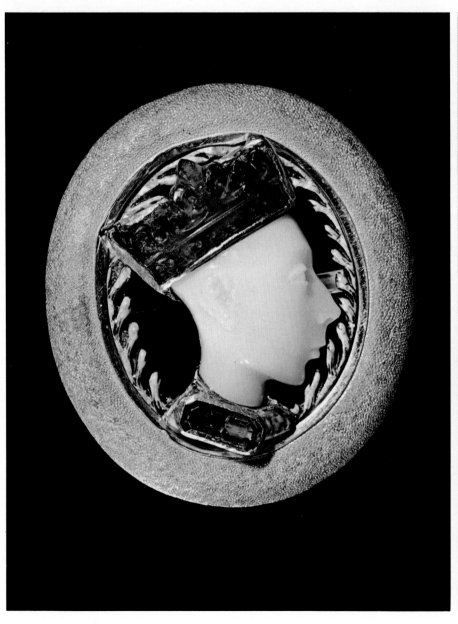

JEAN FOUQUET
Tours ca. 1420—Tours ca. 1480
Portrait of a Man, ca. 1455
Brush with black and gray tones, black chalk,
sanguine, on gray prepared paper;
10^{15}/$_{16}$" x 8^{1}/$_{8}$"

the early French school. Most of them were acquired in 1768 in Brussels
as part of Count Carl Cobentzl's huge collection of Western European
drawings, which became the foundation of the Hermitage's own graphics
collection. After the famous collections in France itself, the Hermitage's
collection of French crayon drawings is one of the largest and most varied
in the world. Those dating from the 15th century are relatively rare, and
the Hermitage possesses only one from this period, the portrait of a man
in a tall hat, attributed to the great French artist, Jean Fouquet.

The apparent simplicity of Fouquet's portraits invariably belies the depth
of their contents. The man's large head, turned in three-quarter profile,
takes up almost the entire sheet, giving the impression that the space allot-
ted is not adequate—the crown and the brim of the hat are cut short and
the shoulders only briefly indicated. The face, with its large nose and small
eyes, is faithfully and straightforwardly drawn, without any idealization. It
is not a beautiful face, but one with an intelligent, energetic look.

Fouquet, as if anticipating the style of crayon portraiture which was to ap-

pear in France in the next century, introduces the effect of color into his
drawings. Contributing to the polychrome effect in this drawing is the gray-
ish tone with which the surface of the paper is prepared.

UNKNOWN ARTIST—LATE SIXTEENTH CENTURY. *Portrait of an Unknown Man.*

For over two hundred years this portrait was believed to represent the Duke
of Alençon and was attributed to François Clouet. However, after careful
examination of the painting (based on the style, the historical documentary
evidence, and laboratory tests) the experts of the Hermitage agreed to ex-
clude both names. For one thing, the delicate and ethereal painting, built
up by a very fine use of tone, using only two or three colors, with trans-

parent modeling and evanescent chiaroscuro, is essentially very different from Clouet's technique. Untypical of Clouet also is the psychological approach and the careful attention to the facial expression, with its steady yet evasive gaze, and the slightly cold, ironic smile. Although this work is of a completely different style and technique, it cannot be said to be inferior to Clouet's work. Among the French 16th-century portraitists, however, there is one whose work closely resembles this painting. This artist is known for a series of exquisite portraits in pencil, all unsigned except one which is inscribed "Master I.D.C."

104

CLAUDE LORRAIN
Chamagne 1600—Rome 1682
Landscape with Apollo and the Sybil of Cumae (The Gulf of Baia)
Oil on canvas; 29³/₁₆″ x 49¼″
Two strips, each 1¹³/₁₆″ wide, which were made and added to the left and right sides of the painting when it was in the Walpole collection between 1720 and 1755, are no longer there. The authenticity of the painting is without question, as Claude's own sketch of it is in the *Liber Veritatis*—the artist's catalogue of his own works, under the heading "No. 99 B"

JEAN-ANTOINE WATTEAU
Valenciennes 1684—Nogent-sur-Marne 1721
Actors of the Théâtre Français
Oil on canvas; 7¹³⁄₁₆″ x 9⅞″
The painting shows actors from the Théâtre
Français in Dancourt's *Three Cousins,* which
provided the inspiration for several of Watteau's
paintings. On the left is Christine Antoinette
Demar, one of the leading actresses of the time,
a huge success in both tragic and comic roles
(depicted in many of Watteau's pictures). The
young man in the beret is Philippe Poisson,
Mme. Demar's usual partner. The other girl
remains unidentified. The old man on the right
is Pierre le Noir la Tortillière, son of a well-
known actor in Molière's troupe, who usually
played comic roles or those of servants.

FRANÇOIS CLOUET. *Portrait of Charles IX.* *p. 103*
Crayon portraits were very popular in 16th-century French art. Compara-
tively cheap and portable, they were in great demand among the French nobility. The portraits of the second half of the century are distinguished from
earlier examples by more precise and detailed draughtsmanship. Although
the model, as before, is shown in a three-quarters profile, half-length portraits started to appear, and greater attention was paid to details of dress.
Charles IX (1550–1574), son of Catherine de' Medici and Henry II, became
King of France in 1560. His reign was marked by the bloody events of St.
Bartholomew's Night (1572). The Hermitage drawing shows Charles IX as
a youth of sixteen, but his troubled gaze and tightly compressed lips already
tell us a good deal about his suspicious and cruel character.

105

CLAUDE LORRAIN. *Landscape with Apollo and the Sybil of Cumae (The Gulf of Baia).* p. 104

Claude Lorrain's painting, which unites a delicate lyricism with the severity of Classical canons, is among the highest achievements of 17th-century European landscape painting. Although Claude's aim was always to faithfully depict nature, he quite often adds a poetic or philosophical aura to his landscape, by introducing literary, religious or mythological themes. In the *Gulf of Baia,* the artist takes his inspiration from an episode in Ovid's *Metamorphoses* (XIV, 135–150). Apollo, who is in love with the Sybil of Cumae, offers to grant her anything she wishes. Taking a handful of sand, the Sybil asks him to give her as many years of life as there are grains of sand in her palm, forgetting to ask for perpetual youth throughout those years.

The themes of death, immortality and the passage of time, which are woven into Ovid's poems, are reflected in Claude's landscapes. Nature in all her beauty and majesty is the embodiment of all that is eternal and fugitive. The great buildings he depicts are all in ruins, and overgrown with ivy and scrub (he introduced in his landscape the Roman aqueduct of Aqua Marzia and the ruins of a building that suggests the Colosseum). These ruins are there to remind us that everything created by man will sooner or later disappear from the face of the earth. People and their passions are also mere mortals, as the figures of Apollo and the Sybil, so dwarfed by the great landscape around them, remind us.

JEAN-ANTOINE WATTEAU. *Actors of the Théâtre Français.* p. 105

From his earliest years, Watteau had always loved the theatre. His quick sketches, done during theatrical performances, are well known, as are his many paintings inspired by the theatre. Although these works are all very different, according to tradition they all go under the general title of *Scenes from the Theatre.* Until recently the picture in the Hermitage was also considered to be one of these. Watteau himself never named any of his pictures; this was done later by different catalogue compilers and engravers, so that at different times, and for different reasons this picture was called *After the Ball, Before the Ball, Flirtatious Girls,* and finally, *Actors from the Italian Theatre.* The last name was based on the fact that the characters are said to be wearing Italian costumes. Detailed study of the picture, however, indicates that is is a rare example of a group portrait by Watteau.

JEAN-BAPTISTE-SIMÉON CHARDIN. *Grace Before the Meal (La Bénédicité).*

Chardin was one of the major exponents of the realistic movement in 18th-century France before the Revolution. Despite the fact that Chardin's work was not in the then predominant Rococo style, his pictures were extremely popular among his contemporaries. With warmth and profound understanding, he depicted the lives of ordinary people—the lower middle class and the craftsmen—contrasting their daily preoccupations with the careless and thoughtless frittering away of time by the aristocracy. *Grace Before the Meal* is one of these pictures, and also one where Chardin is at his best.

Everything in the picture is painted with the same care, the same eye for detail. Color, form and essence of each and every object or figure are faithfully reproduced. Nothing was too small for his studied attention.

JEAN-BAPTISTE-SIMÉON CHARDIN
Paris 1699—Paris 1779
Grace before the Meal (*La Bénédicité*)
Oil on canvas; 19½" x 15⅛"
Signed lower left: *"Chardin 1744"*
Chardin never made preparatory sketches for his paintings, making changes during the course of the work. He returned several times to this subject. Some versions differ only slightly from this one; in one, the composition is extended to the left and the figure of a boy-servant appears, in another the mother is seated. The Hermitage version is more subtle in tone, and this is the one in the series to which the painter added his name.

JEAN-BAPTISTE PERRONNEAU
Paris 1715—Amsterdam 1783
Portrait of a Boy with a Book, 1745–1746
Oil on canvas; 24¹³⁄₁₆″ x 20½″

JEAN-BAPTISTE PERRONNEAU. *Portrait of a Boy with a Book.*
Perronneau was one of the best-known portrait painters of the 18th century.
He received commissions as much from members of high society as from
the bourgeoisie. His favorite medium was pastel. The *Portrait of a Boy with
a Book* was done in oils, but has the softness of color and facture of pastel.
The boy's character is depicted with great objectivity—frail, unsure, his
thoughts are miles away. This is one of the finest examples of a child's portrait by Perronneau. The boy is probably the artist's young brother. In the
1746 Salon catalogue, there is an entry which reads: "Portrait in oils of a
schoolboy with a book, the artist's brother." It is highly probable that this
refers to the picture now in the Hermitage. We know of one other picture
by the same artist of a boy with a book (in the Jacques Doucet collection
at the end of the 19th century), but this one is in pastels and shows a child
of about four or five years old, who could hardly be described as a schoolboy. In the 18th century, the picture was classed among those of unknown
artists, then in the 19th attributed to Greuze and later to Lépicié.

ÉTIENNE-MAURICE FALCONET
Paris 1716—Paris 1791
Flora, ca. 1770
Marble; height 12⁹/₁₆″
The Hermitage *Flora* was executed in Russia
around 1770 for Prince Yusupov, although his
first model of the subject dates back a number of
years, between 1750 and 1760.

ÉTIENNE-MAURICE FALCONET. *Flora.*
Before his stay in Russia and the completion of his celebrated statue of Peter I *(" The Bronze Horseman")* in Petersburg, Falconet was known mainly
for his exquisite statuettes in marble and bronze. He spent a good ten years
working at the Sèvres porcelain factory. He had the rare gift of being able
to combine precision and clarity of thought with elegance of form. In his
works grace never turns into superficial airs, nor does lyricism ever become
insipid. His goddesses, nymphs and bathers are charming young girls, captured in a moment of unconstrained and graceful movement.
The small figurine of the seated Flora is characteristic of the artist's work.
In ancient mythology, Flora is the goddess of spring and flowers. She is often depicted with flowers in her hands and a little garland on her head. Falconet's *Flora* is captivating because of her youthfulness, grace and soft,
coquettish femininity. With its masterfully composed spatial organization
and harmoniously flowing line, this finely and delicately modeled figure is
one of the sculptor's most poetic interpretations of this theme.

Left
JEAN-HONORÉ FRAGONARD
Grasse 1732—Paris 1806
The Snatched Kiss, 1750s
Oil on canvas; 17¾" x 21⅝"
In the 1770s and 1780 it became the fashion for French artists to paint pictures "in series." Greuze, for example, built up a whole story in this way. Fragonard painted a companion picture to the one in the Hermitage which represents *The Marriage Contract,* the next step in the lives of the two people in this painting.

GABRIEL DE SAINT-AUBIN
Paris 1724—Paris 1780
Fashionable Society in the Park, 1760–1761
Pen with brown and black ink, combined with brown and gray washes, gouache, and watercolor; 12⅜" x 10⅛"
One of the artist's favorite subjects was people strolling in parks and along streets. In the years 1760–61 Gabriel de Saint-Aubin executed various versions of this theme, in paintings which are now in the National Gallery, London, and the Perpignan Museum, and drawings which are now in the Netherlands Institute in Paris, and in the Hermitage. There is an engraving of the drawing, by A. J. Duclos.

Right
JEAN-BAPTISTE GREUZE
Tournus 1725—Paris 1805
Young Woman in an Armchair, ca. 1765
Black chalk; 15¹⁵⁄₁₆" x 12¹³⁄₁₆"
The drawing is a preparatory study for the mother in the painting titled *The Adored Mother* (de Labord collection, Paris).
The Hermitage possesses five other studies for this same painting, among which are the figure of the father, the eldest daughter and the baby hiding his face on the mother's knees. There is a study for the grandmother in the Louvre, Paris, and the sketch for the whole composition in the Albertina, Vienna.

JEAN HONORÉ FRAGONARD. *The Snatched Kiss.*   *p. 110*

The Snatched Kiss is one of Fragonard's most charming works, painted during his later, mature period. Under the influence of leading artists like Greuze and Chardin, and also of the 17th-century Dutch masters, Fragonard painted several realistic genre scenes of contemporary life, among which is *The Snatched Kiss.* The girl's startled look, the youth's impromptu action, their mutual glee, are all caught and crystallized on the canvas. The silk of the girl's dress, the transparency of her light scarf, the high polish of the little table, the velvety texture of the carpet are all depicted with extraordinary accuracy in the Dutch manner. In spite of this, there is no lack either of Fragonard's inimitable unconstraint or his delicacy of execution.

GABRIEL DE SAINT-AUBIN. *Fashionable Society in the Park.*   *p. 111*

18th-century France was replete with brilliant painters who were also magnificent draughtsmen and watercolorists. F. Boucher, J.-H. Fragonard, H. Robert, J.-B. Greuze are only a few of the outstanding draughtsmen of the time, among whom Gabriel de Saint-Aubin was a shining light.

Saint-Aubin's talents covered many aspects of drawing, from quick sketches to large, finished compositions. He did sketches from life, and had a predilection for theater and genre scenes; they were executed in black chalk and sanguine, with pen and brush, gouache and watercolor—he mastered all these different techniques.

Fashionable Society in the Park is one of the gems of the Hermitage's collection of French drawings, exquisite in its diminutive dimensions. Saint-Aubin's drawings are nearly monochrome, yet they possess surprising nuances of color. Employing a combination of black, brown, and white washes, with touches of watercolor, the artist manages to achieve an inimitable play of mauve, yellow-greenish and bluish tones.

JEAN-BAPTISTE GREUZE. *Young Woman in an Armchair.*   *p. 111*

The Hermitage possesses the largest collection in the world of drawings by Greuze, numbering 125 sheets. It is known that before painting a picture, Greuze always did a great deal of preparatory work, particularly a large number of life studies. Quite often he repeated the same figure or detail several times with slight variations. He always advised young artists to make several sketches and studies before taking up their brushes.

The picture entitled *Adored Mother* (De Labord Collection, Paris), is a portrait of the Labord family. The Hermitage drawing is a preparatory study for the figure of the mother, Madame de Labord.

This study of the young woman is one of the finest of Greuze's works in the Hermitage. The limited black and white tones of the drawing harmonize nicely with the refined figure and pose of the model. Her gentle expression, silky hair and the folds of her dress are masterfully rendered in a sweeping, captivating harmony of stroke.

JACQUES-LOUIS DAVID. *Sappho and Phaon.*

A painter of historical scenes and portraits, the founder and leading exponent of French Classicism, David was commissioned to paint *Sappho and*

JACQUES-LOUIS DAVID
Paris 1748—Brussels 1825
Sappho and Phaon
Oil on canvas; 88¼" x 103⅜"
Signed and dated lower left: *"L. David 1809"*

Phaon by Prince N. Yusupov, a Russian art collector. The choice of subject was left to the artist, and he chose one of the legends about the life of the ancient Greek poetess, Sappho. In a letter to Prince Yusupov, dated September 22, 1808, David wrote: "I have only just thrown the subject of this picture onto the canvas—it represents the sensitive poetess Sappho and her lover Phaon whom Cupid has finally succeeded in igniting with his fire. You mentioned your intention of coming to see the picture in my studio   113

JEAN-ANTOINE HOUDON
Versailles 1741—Paris 1828
Voltaire Seated in an Armchair
Marble; height 53¼"
Signed and dated: *"Houdon Fecit 1781"*

before leaving the country, so that you can have some idea of what it will look like. If I have been slow in allowing you this pleasure, it is only because I have been waiting for the proper inspiration. I think the moment has finally arrived, but it is you who will be the better judge of this." In a subsequent letter, dated November 30, 1809, David informed the Prince that the picture was completed.

Following the dictates of Classicism, David did not try to instill any feeling of genuine or spontaneous emotion into his picture. The important thing for him was above all the harmony and unity of all the plastic elements of the composition, the purity and perfection of each form, the measured rhythm of the lines, the sonority and balance of the tones.

JEAN-ANTOINE HOUDON. *Voltaire Seated in an Armchair.*   *p. 114*

A wonderfully nostalgic image of Voltaire (François-Marie Arouet, 1694–1778), the celebrated French writer, philosopher and critic, has been left us by his contemporary, the sculptor Houdon. This life-size statue of Voltaire seated is the best of the artist's portraits of him. The great philosopher posed for Houdon at the great age of eighty-four. The sculptor faithfully reproduced every feature, every wrinkle on the face, the dry fingers, the toothless mouth. Yet Houdon managed to produce a true work of genius; we see before us in the Hermitage not just an ordinary old man, but the incarnation of the crowning genius of his century. An inner flame somehow illuminates his whole being, and makes every muscle seem alive. Through the ironic smile, the attentive and penetrating glance, the life-force which makes itself felt in the feeble body, Houdon expresses the triumph of an indestructible spirit over the already failing flesh.

While portraying the psychology and character of Voltaire, Houdon also sought to typify the man as a philosopher—thus his old housecoat draped around him becomes like an ancient toga, hiding his thinness. All that is showing are his almost ghost-like hands and his head crowned with the fillet of a Greek philosopher.

The statue is remarkable not only for its psychology, but also for the extraordinary finish of the marble, through which Houdon with extreme realism succeeded in conveying the soft, old skin, the texture of the material, the malicious and penetrating gaze of the philosopher.

JEAN-AUGUSTE-DOMINIQUE INGRES. *Portrait of a Young Woman.*

In contrast to Ingres' strictly classical compositions, often rather artificial and cold, this drawing is simple, honest and full of that "higher truthfulness in art" which the artist himself always demanded of his work. The ability of one single free, sweeping and at the same time absolutely precise line to capture the entire form, makes every single stroke individual and expressive. This is the case in this drawing, in which the artist not only portrays the girl's attractive external appearance, but also her inner purity. The similarity between this drawing and one of the figures in the group portrait of the family of Lucien Bonaparte (brother of Napoleon), leads us to conclude that our drawing is a study for the preparatory drawing for the composition (Fogg Museum, Cambridge, Mass.). The figure of the girl standing almost in the center of the composition, immediately behind Alexandrina Bonaparte (Lucien's wife), is in almost exactly the same pose as the girl in the Hermitage drawing. Furthermore, they both have identical hairstyles, shape of face and mouth, and, which is also significant, they are both drawn in the same manner. The identity of the girl, nevertheless, remains a mystery. Experts have produced a variety of theories about who she is; some say that she is Laetitia Bonaparte (Alexandrina and Lucien's daughter); others, that she is Anna Guberton, Alexandrina's daughter from her first marriage; and still others that she is Christina Bonaparte, the daughter of Lucien and Christina Boyer.

EUGÈNE DELACROIX. *Lion Hunt in Morocco.*   *p. 117*

This picture is one of the most important in the series of hunting pictures which Delacroix painted in his later years. The artist concentrates on the dynamism and expressiveness of pose and gesture rather than accuracy of drawing and form. The excitement of the lion hunt is conveyed to us through sharply contrasted colors, and through the uneven, free and generous brush strokes. Despite the fact that the picture is not based on an actual impression but on the artist's creative imagination, and despite the fact that the rules of proportion and perspective have been cast aside, the figures of the hunters are full of life and vitality.

An entry in Delacroix's diary would seem to refer to this picture. On April 23, 1854, the artist wrote: "The study I made of the trees along my road has helped me to return to the picture of the *Lion Hunters,* which in my bad frame of mind yesterday I had got into an unfortunate state, although it had been going well the day before. I was seized with inspired rage, like the other day when I reworked the *Clorinde,* not that there were changes to be made, but the picture had gotten into that languishing and dull state which simply points a finger at lack of ardor in working. I feel sorry for the people who work tranquilly and coldly." Finally on June 22 of that same year, the painter noted: "I have finished the canvases of *The Arab on the Lookout for a Lion,* and *Women at the Fountain.*" Although Delacroix gave various titles to his works, this is probably a reference to the same canvas, date 1854, which is today in the Hermitage.

JEAN-FRANÇOIS MILLET. *Death and the Peasant.*   *p. 118*
This drawing is one of a pair of known studies for the painting entitled *Death and the Woodcutter,* dated 1858–59 (Carlsberg Gliptothek, Copenhagen), the subject of which is taken from the La Fontaine fable of the same name. The image of the peasant's heavy, painful work runs like a thread through many of Millet's works. For him, the beauty and poetry of life was to be found in the fate of man that he wins his daily bread "in the sweat of his brow." This theme haunted Millet and he returned to it in many of his paintings, either in paintings inspired by the everyday life of the peasants, or in allegorical compositions like the one for which this drawing is a design. The particular value of this drawing lies in the fact that it enables us to see the structural and metaphorical development of the composition. Millet did not utter empty words when he said that the meaning of a painting should be immediately apparent and not be diverted by anything else. Indeed, this summary sketch already contains all the elements that he was later to incorporate in the painting—the positioning of the figures, the distribution of movement, even the layout of the landscape. The emotional resonance of the allegorical subject likewise remains unchanged from the drawing to the painting, the man's weariness and his fate being expressed in the painting with somber colors very much in keeping with the black crayon of the drawing.

EDGAR DEGAS. *After the Bath.*   *p. 119*
The woman in this picture is in a pose quite often used by Degas. (Apart from various paintings, he also produced a bronze version in 1896–1911). This picture was painted around 1895. The preparatory study, now in the Georges Viaud collection in Paris, still has traces of the original horizontal and vertical lines on it corresponding to those seen here. However, as the work proceeded, he added two more lines, one at the right and one above.

EUGÈNE DELACROIX
Charenton-Saint-Maurice 1798—Paris 1863
Lion Hunt in Morocco
Oil on canvas; 29⅛" x 36¼"
Signed and dated lower right: *"Eug. Delacroix
1854"*

Moreover, the study lacks the richly colored background. The colors of the
Hermitage picture are bold and original. The emphasis is placed on such
details as the red hair against the yellow-ochre background, the relationship
between the ochre tones of the body and the foamy effect of the towel, and
the violet-colored armchair.

Degas had no need of mythology as an excuse to portray female nudes, although he did once confess that had he been born earlier, he would have
painted Susanna bathing, and not a woman in a bathtub. However, it is not
celebrated goddesses or beauties who appear in Degas' work, but rather his
own, ordinary contemporaries. Their proportions do not conform to the old
pattern, they never pose and so never look elegant in a studied way. Degas
wanted to depict them as they were with natural gestures and movements,   117

not emotively charged poses. Whether he portrays dancers or jockeys, laundresses or women at their dressing tables, they are all equally uncomplicated and natural.

AUGUSTE RODIN. *The Poet and the Muse.*   *p. 120*

All of Rodin's works are impregnated with joy and love of life, a deep interest in all his fellow men, a careful study of their inner world, and a true understanding of their feelings and emotions. The leading sculptor at the turn of the century, he was attracted most of all by heroic, elevated, and dramatic images; but this did not diminish his understanding of and ability to capture the finer shades of human emotion. The theme of love, of artistic creation, and images from literature are often the subject of his works.

In the Hermitage group, the Poet is shown plunged deep in thought. The Muse is a very young girl with a slender, supple body, who in a flowing movement frees herself from the deep sleep binding her, while the Poet, sitting next to her, seems almost to be listening to the beating of her heart. The sculptor imparts a peculiar softness to the marble, blurring the outlines and effacing any sharp division between figures and background. With the boundaries of form thus dissolved, the figures seem to float in ethereal space. This procedure, although typical of Rodin's style, was not his primary aim, but it gives his work a special feeling of poetry, an atmosphere of dreams and deep thought.

JEAN-FRANÇOIS MILLET
Gruchy 1817—Barbizon 1875
Death and the Peasant, 1858
Crayon on yellowish paper; 8⅞" x 14¹/₁₆"
Signed lower left: *"J.F.M."*

EDGAR DEGAS
Paris 1834—Paris 1917
After the Bath, ca. 1895
Pastel and gouache on board; 32½" x 28⅛"
Signed above right: *"degas"*
The pose of the figure in this pastel is found in a number of works by the artist—besides various versions of the years 1896–1911 there is also a bronze statuette.

118

AUGUSTE RODIN
Paris 1840—Meudon 1917
The Poet and the Muse, 1905
Marble; height 24¹³/₁₆″
The theme of love and of artistic creativity, as well as images evoked from literature are frequent subjects in Rodin's works.

PAUL CÉZANNE. *Mont Sainte-Victoire.*   *p. 121*

There is no theme that Cézanne loved more than Mont Sainte-Victoire, which he saw out of his studio window and painted again and again. For him this mountain stood for all the magnificence, simplicity and indestructibility of nature. Cézanne's habit of working "around the motif" very often meant working around the Mont Sainte-Victoire; in contrast to the Impressionists, he always sought definitive form.

In the Hermitage picture, Mont Sainte-Victoire is such a dominating element that all the rest of the landscape is subordinate, yielding to the rhythms which it imposes. Cézanne does not sacrifice his picture to optical exactness. Both the linear and atmospheric rules of perspective are broken—the mountain is too much in relief and excessively close to the observer. Yet even with such proximity, many details are omitted. The modeling of the mountain itself becomes the plastic theme of the picture.

PAUL GAUGUIN. *Conversation (Parau Parau).*   *p. 122*

During his first eighteen months on Tahiti, Gauguin painted about fifty canvases, but he considered that only nine of these would be of any interest to the European public as examples of his new direction. The first of these works, which was sent to a Copenhagen exhibition on the 8th of December 1892, was this picture, *Parau Parau.* In a letter to his wife, the artist translated the title as *"Parole, Parole"* (Words, Words), and in a letter to Daniel de Monfreid as *"Conversation, ou les Potins"* (Conversation, or Gossip). There is some confusion whether this was the actual painting sent to Copenhagen, as another later version (1892) exists under the same title. This

PAUL CÉZANNE
Aix-en-Provence 1839—Aix-en-Provence 1906
Mont Sainte-Victoire, 1896–1898
Oil on canvas; 30¼″ x 15¼″
Experts on Cézanne are not all in agreement on
the date of this canvas, but most concur with
Rewald on the date 1896–1898. Later, around
1904, Cézanne painted another view of Mont
Sainte-Victoire (now in the Cleveland Museum
of Art), in the foreground of which are some
umbrella pines and the road to Toulon.

is now in the Whitney Collection, New York. However, the unity of composition, with the attention directed at a group of ordinary, yet rather enigmatic Tahitians, whom the artist tried to portray just as they were, as opposed to the European artists' custom of using exotic Parisian models, leads us to suggest that it was in fact this picture (i.e., the one in the Hermitage), which went to Copenhagen. This opinion is given further credence by the fact that Gauguin himself wrote the titles in Tahitian on his paintings (as he mentioned in his letters to his wife and to Monfreid), and there is some doubt whether the handwriting on the later picture is in fact his.

But quite apart from the question of whether or not this picture was shown at the exhibition, the artist, trying to make the public interested in the secret hidden in these foreign words, nevertheless created a simple and natural composition, which he obviously copied straight from life. The theme of the picture is not a genre theme, but rather a pictorial representation of the atmosphere and the calm, unhurried way of life on the island, the age-long natural harmony between Man and Nature.

PIERRE AUGUSTE RENOIR. *Portrait of the Actress Jeanne Samary.*
This is the most important of all the portraits ever done of this famous Co-
médie Française actress, whose life was tragically short (1857–1890). It was
painted for the Salon of 1879, and this explains why the canvas is more conventional and traditional than his other portraits of Jeanne Samary. However, even though he was aiming at official approval and success, the artist
still managed to avoid the worst of the tricks and falsities which were so
much part of the Salon style.

This work was preceded by four other portraits of Samary, painted in 1877;
and in the following year Renoir painted yet another—a small half-length
portrait of the actress—which is now in a private collection in Switzerland
and appears to be the immediate predecessor to the Hermitage version.

Jeanne's captivating smile, the wonderful effect of the pink froth of her
dress against the dark background, the natural pose—everything speaks of
the charm of youth and beauty under the spell of which Renoir was to fall
so readily. In later years, Renoir was to recall Jeanne Samary, saying:
"What an entrancing girl! What beautiful skin—literally radiant!"

PAUL GAUGUIN
Paris 1848—Atuana, Marquesas Islands, 1903
Conversations (Parau, Parau)
Oil on canvas; 26⅜" x 36⁷/₁₆"
Inscribed lower left: *"Les Parau Parau—
P. Gauguin 91"*
In a letter to his wife, the artist translated the
title as *"Parole, Parole"* (Words, Words); and in
a letter to Daniel de Monfried, as *"Conversation,
ou les Potins"* (Conversation, or Gossip). There
is some question whether this was the actual
painting sent to Copenhagen, or another later
version, dating from 1892 (now in the Whitney
Collection, New York).

PIERRE-AUGUSTE RENOIR
Limoges 1841—Cagnes 1919
Portrait of the Actress Jeanne Samary
Oil on canvas; 68⅛″ x 40½″
Signed and dated lower left: *"Renoir 78"*
According to the artist's son Jean, her parents
were great admirers of Renoir's work and
proposed to have him paint their daughter. The
artist worked on the portrait in his studio in the
Rue Saint-Georges with great enthusiasm. It was
said that he was always so keen to start painting
that he would neglect to greet her on arrival.

HENRI MATISSE. *The Dance.*

The idea for this famous decoration, comprising two panels (together with *Music,* also in the Hermitage), gradually crystallized over a period of five years. In composition, *The Dance* is similar to *The Joy of Life,* 1905–1906 (Barnes Foundation, Merion, Pa.), in which a round dance is shown in the background. In the beginning of spring 1909, when Matisse was working on the first version of *The Dance* (Museum of Modern Art, New York), Serge Shchukin, who already had some of Matisse's works in his collection, commissioned a panel on the same theme for the stairwell of his private residence in Moscow. The watercolor study for *The Dance,* given to Shchukin by Matisse, is now in the Pushkin Museum of Fine Arts, Moscow.

The apparent simplicity of *The Dance* hides a complicated web of thoughts and associations. Having set the piece in the far distant mythological dawn of mankind, Matisse produced a metaphorical structure charged with symbolic meaning. Scholars specializing in primitive cultures tell us that dances in which people all hold hands symbolize the unity of earth and sky. And in Matisse's dionysiac round dance the earth and the sky are not merely the background, but an integral part of the action.

HENRI MATISSE
Le Cateau 1869—Nice 1954
Oil on canvas; 102⁵/₁₆″ x 153⁷/₈″
Signed and dated lower right: *"Henri Matisse 1910"*
In an interview published in the Paris newspaper *Les Nouvelles,* April 12, 1909, Matisse explained his idea for the great decorative scheme he intended to realize for the Shchukin palace in Moscow: "I have a stairwell to decorate. It is three stories high. I put myself in the place of a visitor arriving from outdoors. He finds himself on the first floor. Some gesture of greeting must be made, a feeling of ease imparted. My first panel represents a dance, that wild round taking place on a hilltop. On the second floor the heart of the house is reached; in its spirit and silence I imagine a scene of music with attentive listeners . . . I plan to realize all this in the simplest way and with the most primal, irreducible means, those which allow an artist to express his interior vision with perfect relevance."

GERMAN, ENGLISH, SPANISH ART

XV—XX centuries

LUCAS CRANACH THE ELDER. *Venus and Cupid.*   *p. 127*

Lucas Cranach the Elder, one of the greatest artists of the German Renaissance, embodied in his *Venus* his view of the ideal of feminine beauty and perfect proportions of the human body. His picture is the first example in Northern European art of depicting the classical goddess nude. Cranach's Venus is a tall woman, slightly angular, with long legs and a small head. The gentle rhythm and smooth, flowing lines of the figure, which Cranach inherited from late Gothic art, give her an appealing expressiveness.

Venus and Cupid indicates the artist's wide range of interests and his sympathy with the humanistic ideas spreading through Germany in the 16th century. Cranach gives us the German interpretation of one of the popular themes of the Italian Renaissance. For Italian artists, Venus was the quintessence of sensual beauty, boldly and openly celebrated with her naked body. Cranach's picture has a moralistic air, warning the onlooker against sweet temptation in a Latin verse inscribed at the top of the picture: "Try with all your might to ignore Cupid's voluptuousness/ Otherwise Venus will take hold of your poor, blind soul."

The coloring of the painting is fairly uniform, confined to yellow and golden tones. The only bright accent is the necklace of red beads around Cupid's neck.

There are numerous versions of this picture both by Cranach himself and by his pupils, disciples and imitators.

In 1509 Cranach produced a wood engraving of the subject which differed in a few details from the painting, and had a landscape background.

HANS HOLBEIN THE ELDER [?]. *Portrait of the Artist's Sons Ambrosius and Hans the Younger.*   *p. 128*

On the right is the artist's eldest son, Ambrosius, and on the left his youngest, Hans. The town depicted below is a view of Augsburg. A dwarf similar to the one appearing in this drawing is found in another Hans Holbein the Elder drawing, now in a private collection in Paris (Glaser, No. 99).

A comparison between this drawing and another, now in the Kupferstichkabinett in West Berlin (inv. No. 2507), dated 1511 and also showing the artist's sons—where they appear younger—enables us to date the Hermitage work as approximately 1514.

The painstaking care and rather dry execution of this drawing leads us to believe that this may well be a copy, made perhaps by one of his sons, and that the original is no longer in existence. Franz Winzinger tends toward attributing the work to Hans Holbein the Younger, and consequently dates it from the period just before Hans the Younger left Augsburg for Basel. He also refutes the idea that this is a portrait of Hans the Elder's sons.

LUCAS CRANACH THE ELDER
Kronach 1472—Weimar 1553
Venus and Cupid
Oil on canvas, transferred from wood;
83¹³⁄₁₆″ x 40⅛″
Signed at left center: *"LC"* with the insignia of
the dragon and the date.

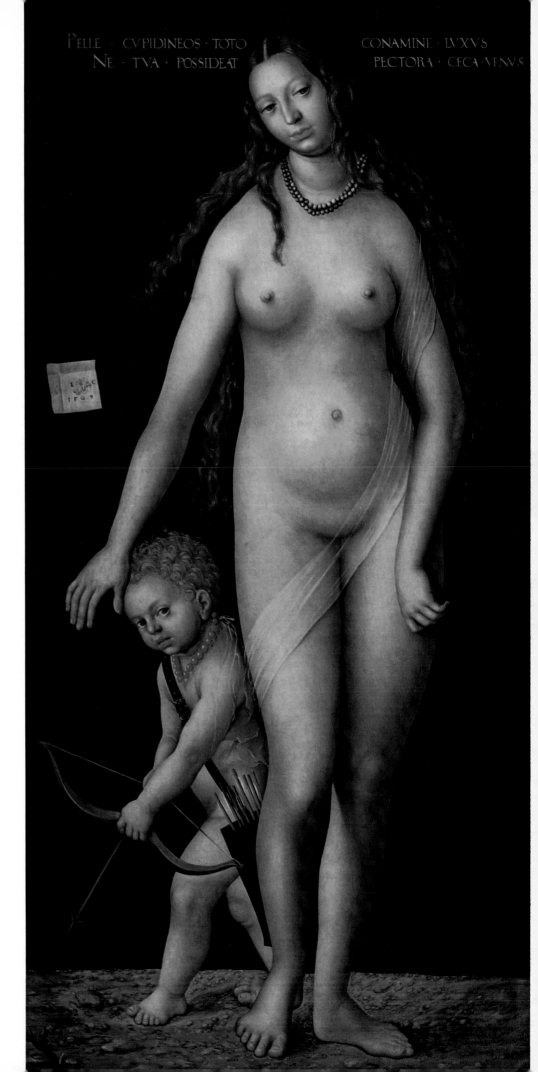

PELLE · CVPIDINEOS · TOTO   CONAMINE · LVXVS
NE · TVA · POSSIDEAT   PECTORA · CECA · VENVS

ALBRECHT DÜRER. *Allegory of Justice.* p. 129
This drawing from life, executed as a study of folds of the mantle, served as a preliminary sketch for Dürer's engraving *The Sun of Justice.* This engraving is based on the ancient concept of the sun-god as the supreme judge. According to Erwin Panofsky, the literary source of this idea might be a work of the Benedictine monk, Petrus Berkhorius, entitled *Repertorium morale,* which was published by Anton Koberger in Nuremberg about the time of this drawing.

Dürer had already used the Hermitage study in the design for the composition (Kupferstichkabinett, Dresden) of the engraving. In that design, the allegorical figure of Justice is sitting on a lion—a motif which reflects the old astrological belief of the relationships between the planets and the signs of the zodiac.

In the Hermitage drawing, Dürer's style is not yet entirely free of Gothic influence, showing the artist still searching for the limpid clarity of line and form of the Renaissance.

128

HANS HOLBEIN THE ELDER
Augsburg ca. 1465—Isenheim 1524
Portrait of the Artist's Sons Ambrosius and Hans the Younger, ca. 1514
Silverpoint on white prepared paper;
4⅞" x 6⁷⁄₁₆"

ALBRECHT DÜRER
Nuremberg 1471—Nuremberg 1528
Allegory of Justice
Pen and black ink; 9½" x 8³⁄₁₆"

129

GERMAN ART. *The Madonna with the Archangel Michael and a Saint.*
The Madonna, who occupies the center of the composition, is portrayed
with all the attributes of her sanctity—the crown, the aureole, the crescent
moon. The Archangel Michael at left is shown weighing a soul and its
works. This motif is frequent in medieval art and is introduced here with
entertaining ingenuity, merging embroidery with popular art. The standing
youth at right is depicted with equal vivacity.
Unlike early medieval works in which the background has neither depth
nor concrete elements, here the lower part of the composition is divided
into small oblique squares, suggesting a floor. The date of execution is embroidered twice: in Old Gothic and in Latin script.

GERMAN ART. *Deer-hunt Tapestry.*   *p. 131*
The so-called "*spaliers*" or woven rugs without nap—i.e., tapestries—which
hung on walls and whose manufacture was already known in the eleventh
and twelfth centuries in Western Europe, were widely used in the Middle
Ages to decorate residences and churches. Biblical and evangelical subjects,
and scenes from the times of chivalry were represented on them and were
interpreted fairly conventionally, flatly and decoratively.
These characteristics are exemplified in this German deer-hunt tapestry, of
which various versions are known. In medieval art, the deer appears as the
embodiment of faithfulness, and its representation here and in other versions can be interpreted as an allegory of the pursuit of this virtue.

GERMAN ART
Madonna with Archangel Michael and a Saint
1477
Embroidered linen and wool; 35⁷/₁₆″ x 72⁷/₁₆″

130

GERMAN ART
Deer-hunt Tapestry
Alsace, end of XV century—beginning
of XVI century
Wool, silk, gold thread: 30¼″ x 34¼″

131

WOLF EISPINGER. *Wedding Cup.*
Goblets in the form of a female figure—*Jungfrau*—were made as wedding cups. This kind of cup could also be used upside down for bride and groom to drink out of in turn. The ornamentation of similar goblets was very varied. Here almost all the surface is decorated with engraved floral designs.

MONOGRAMMIST IP. *Mourning for Christ.*   *p. 133*
This relief is one of the few surviving examples of the work of the so-called Monogrammist IP, an artist of the Danube school active in the region of Salzburg. The particular fascination of the works of this school is the wonderful harmony between man and nature. The rationality and strict obser-

WOLF EISPINGER
Wedding Cup
End of XVI century
Chased silver gilt; height 10″
Nuremberg provenance

MONOGRAMMIST IP
Active between 1520 and 1530
Mourning for Christ, ca. 1520–1525
Boxwood; 7¹¹⁄₁₆″ x 6⅛″
Initials of the artist, bottom center: *"IP"*

vance of form in this composition show the influence of the Italian Renaissance. Despite its small dimensions, the work is monumental in its treatment of the subject. The mastery of the sculptor is also evident in the use of powerful foreshortening. Notwithstanding the great beauty of the composition and the design, this was not the artist's principal aim—the work is imbued with a deep feeling of grief and sorrow.

CASPAR DAVID FRIEDRICH. *On a Sailboat.*   *p. 134*

Friedrich was one of the most important European artists to emerge at the beginning of the 19th century. His work represents all the best features of German Romanticism. It is imbued with the idea of an integral unity between Nature and the spiritual world of Man. This general philosophical idea can be seen in Friedrich's personal outlook, as in this picture, as well as through actual events in the artist's life. Painted in 1818, this canvas is an amazingly bold work for its time, anticipating the achievements of Impressionism. The artist painted himself and his wife on their honeymoon and this painting has a happy, light atmosphere. The extremely detailed and lifelike foreground (Friedrich's travel journals are full of painstakingly detailed studies of sailing ships), contrasts with the background which is illusive, weightless and bewitching—fantasy rather than fact, what is sometimes called "floating architecture." It is precisely this contrast, in addition to the lack of anything to link the background to the foreground which creates the very special, romantic atmosphere, which somehow seems to draw the spectator into the artist's world. But his intention becomes clear when one compares this picture with two others, also in the Hermitage, *Moon Rising over the Sea,* and *The Harbor at Night.* All three works were painted at approximately the same time and form a special sort of romantic triptych, of which *On a Sailboat* is the left wing.
This picture was acquired by the Russian Emperor Nicholas I in 1820 on a visit to Friedrich's studio in Dresden.

THOMAS GAINSBOROUGH. *Portrait of a Lady in Blue.*   *p. 136*

Portrait of a Lady in Blue is one of Gainsborough's most perfect portraits. The charming silvery blue colors have the same effect on the viewer as listening to a virtuoso musician playing a piece of music in which every note contributes to the harmony. The feeling of peace and serenity emanating from the portrait is due to the precision and sense of rhythm with which the graceful feminine figure, with its pale blue, pink, white, light brown and pearl-gray tones, is placed in the rectangle of the canvas. Thanks to this, the coquettish pose of this fashionable lady, holding up her shawl as it falls from her shoulders, takes on an air of refinement and nobility. Gainsborough's light, flowing brush stroke gives the picture an almost indiscernible movement, and brings the charming figure of the young woman to life.
There has never been any doubt about the date of the portrait. The perfection of its execution indicates that it must have been painted at the height of the artist's powers. His preference for blue tones places the picture in the 1770s or 1780s, which the costume and the high hairstyle topped with a

135

THOMAS GAINSBOROUGH
Sudbury 1727—London 1788
Portrait of a Lady in Blue, ca. 1880
Oil on canvas; 29¹⁵/₁₆" x 25³/₁₆"

tiny hat with a ribbon and ostrich feathers would also indicate. The Hermitage acquired the portrait in 1916 from the Khitrov collection. For a long time it was thought to be the portrait of the Duchess of Beaufort, but there has been no positive proof to support this.

JOSEPH WRIGHT. *The Blacksmith's Forge.*   *p. 137*

On April 30, 1776, Wright wrote from Bath the following words to his brother: "I intend going to Derby so that I can paint a seascape or a blacksmith's shop. That should certainly attract the public to any exhibition in the coming season."

The Blacksmith's Forge, a subject which he repeated and varied many times during the period 1771–1776, is one of the most admired works of the artist. Wright's paintings all illustrate his characteristic use of light and shade. In this picture he contrasts the bright light of the fire—the fire itself being hidden behind the bending figure of the blacksmith—with the pale gleam of

JOSEPH WRIGHT
Derby 1734—Derby 1797
The Blacksmith's Forge
Oil on canvas; 41⅛" x 55⅛"

the moon in a troubled sky. The faces of the people are partially illuminated, and the light from the fire plays on the beams and rafters of the forge, emphasizing the darkness of the landscape outside. This contrast between light and dark imparts a romantic air and an almost theatrical feeling to this common everyday scene.

To the left of the anvil, a man is leaning on a staff. This is probably "the idler in the attitude of someone who just wants to kill time," about whom Wright wrote in his notebook when describing the concept of this picture.

In 1774–1775, *The Blacksmith's Forge* came into Catherine II's collection and was the first of three works by the same artist to be exhibited in St. Petersburg.

JAMES COX. *Table Clock with Figures of a Lion and a Rhinoceros.*
The famous English clockmaker James Cox, active in London from 1760 to 1788, was well-known for the intricate musical mechanisms and moving figurines of his clocks.

In the Hermitage clock, the musical mechanism is hidden in the pedestal in the shape of a little agate box decorated with a network of gilt bronze bands. On the front of the pedestal, rosettes made of strass gems are superimposed, which conceal the winding mechanism.

The whimsical interpretation of Oriental subjects and the portrayal of exotic animals confirm the extremely widespread enthusiasm for Chinese art in the 18th century.

PETER TORKLER. *Table Clock in the Form of a Pavilion with a Fountain.*
This clock is constructed to look like a fountain with flowing water. A mechanism hidden in the base sets in motion the "streams" of little crystal bars, and a musical carillon.

The representation of a many-headed dragon and palm trees reflects the enthusiasm for Oriental art. At the same time, the severe straight lines and the gilt-bronze ornamentation are closer to Classical form.

138

Above left
JAMES COX
Table Clock with Figures of a Lion and a Rhinoceros
London, ca. 1780
Gilt bronze, agate; height 21⅞"

Above right
PETER TORKLER
Table Clock in the Form of a Garden Pavilion with a Fountain
London, ca. 1780
Gilt bronze, crystal; height 23⁷⁄₁₆"

JOSE DE RIBERA. *Sant' Onofrio.* *p. 140*

Ribera often chose the legendary saints of the Catholic church as subjects for his work: St. Jerome, St. Paul the hermit, St. Mary of Egypt, St. Onofrio. In his early period he produced works that were emotionally charged, full of vivid expression, sweeping gestures and sharp contrasts of light and shade. The picture in the Hermitage, *Sant' Onofrio,* belongs to the late 1630s, when Ribera's treatment of his subjects became more restrained.

According to legend, St. Onofrio, son of a king, was sent to be educated in a monastery, and having grown up, rejected his birthright and went off into the wilderness. Onofrio lived the life of a hermit for sixty years. Paintings depicting this saint always show him with a crown and scepter to remind us of his royal birth, and also with a skull, the sign of a recluse. This picture is monochrome, its entire range of color based on different tones of gray, brown and olive-green. With great mastery, Ribera has applied his paint in almost transparent layers thus producing the effect of light shining on the surface of the picture.

FRANCISCO DE ZURBARÁN. *Childhood of the Virgin Mary.* *p. 141*

Spanish painters are noted among Western European artists of the 17th century for their portraits of children. Velázquez, Zurbarán, Murillo, all managed to capture the seriousness and the lively spontaneity of children, whether they were painting portraits, or religious or genre paintings. Zurbarán often turned to the theme of Mary's childhood for his inspiration, drawn from the *Pseudo Gospel of Matthew.* The artist first used this theme toward the end of the 1620s and returned to it many times throughout the rest of his life. The version in the Hermitage is one of the later examples, and is distinguished from the earlier ones by the peaceful, intense, concentrated solution of the theme. The figure of the girl stands out against a dark, neutral background, with a minimum of accessories. Mary, having laid her needlework aside, is praying, her face reflecting profound, sincere emotion. Even in this small picture we can feel the monumentality which always distinguishes Zurbarán's work. The composition is static, the figure monolithic, and all the details of the dress depicted in bold masses. Bright, contrasting colors predominate, like medieval paintings or brightly painted wood sculptures (throughout his life, Zurbarán retained a predilection for bright local color, derived from his early experience of painting statues). His work reveals great attention to detail. The eye is immediately drawn to the delicate embroidery on the collar and cuffs of Mary's dress.

DIEGO VELÁZQUEZ. *Portrait of Count Olivares.* *p. 141*

From 1621 to 1643 Don Gaspar de Guzman, Count of Olivares, (1587–1645), was a minister in the Spanish court. Velázquez was frequently called upon to paint his portrait, often in ceremonial costume, as he was a great favorite of Philip IV, and a very powerful man. The painting dates from the late 1630s and marks the dawning of a new era in the artist's work. At that time, Velázquez decided to specialize in formal half-length portraits, concentrating on unveiling the model's personality. The minister's intelligent, predatory face has a tense expression; his eyes have a skeptical rather than confident look; his deathly pale, fat face with its hanging jowls and swollen

eyelids, the great formless nose all create the impression of an aging man whose strength is ebbing. It is altogether a work of impressive power.
The colors are very restrained. The deep yet expressive black of the costume stands out against the olive-green, partially illuminated background. The white collar, drawn with great precision, projects exquisitely. The face is superbly worked with flowing strokes and bold features.

PABLO PICASSO. *Woman Drinking Absinthe.* *p. 142*
This picture was painted in the autumn of 1901 in Paris, although its compositional elements had already been previously developed, using different models. During this short-lived early period, called his "Blue Period," Picasso was much under the influence of Toulouse-Lautrec and Gauguin. Picasso had already painted a woman in a café in Barcelona in 1899–1900. In the summer of 1901 Picasso put on exhibition at Vollard's a picture called *Absinthe* (Jaffe Collection, New York), which was the starting point on the road which led to *Woman Drinking Absinthe*. The model for this picture is not known, although it would seem to be the same woman as the one portrayed in *Woman with a Chignon* (Fogg Art Museum, Harvard Uni-

PABLO PICASSO
Malaga 1881—Mougins 1973
Woman Drinking Absinthe
Oil on canvas; 28¼″ x 21¼″
Signed above right: *"Picasso"*

versity), and also in *Girl with her Hands Crossed on her Breast* (Obersteg Collection, Geneva).

The subject of the café scene, which the Impressionists were so fond of, is treated in an anti-Impressionist manner by Picasso, not only as regards the form, but more essentially as a psychological study of the woman in this canvas. Her whole face expresses loneliness and waiting. Behind her is a wall, in front of her a table—she is surrounded on all sides, wedged into a corner both literally and metaphorically. Her blue dress highlights the unhealthy yellow pallor of her face and hands, which seems to "compress" the figure even more. The dirty red color of the walls not only renders the atmosphere of a cheap café, but also provides a cheerless background, emphasizing the woman's drab existence.

142

RUSSIAN ART

XV—XIX centuries

NOVGOROD SCHOOL. *Saints Theodore Stratelates and Theodore Tiron.*
The Novgorod school has a very special place in Old Russian painting. It differs from the other schools in that the influence of traditional peasant art is very strongly felt—the simplicity of subject matter, the laconic composition, the bright and impulsive colors.

The icon in the Hermitage collection shows two warrior-saints, Theodore Stratelates and Theodore Tiron. The composition is clear and simple. The figures of the warriors are portrayed frontally without unnecessary symbolism. Their poses are identical, which gives a singular rhythm to the composition. The figures are long and remarkably light, endowing them with a feeling both of elegance and of spirituality. The relationship between the outlines of the two figures and the background of the icon is perfect. The fine, dark features of their faces, characteristic of the Novgorod school, are beautifully painted with quite a developed use of light and shade.

The color of the icon is sparkling, pure and remarkably sonorous. The artist has boldly contrasted yellows, reds, browns and greens, among which the cinnabar cape of Theodore Stratelates stands out. The perfection of line, the expressiveness of the figures, the classical simplicity of the composition and the vivacity of the colors all make this a magnificent example of Novgorod school painting in the 15th century.

ART OF MOSCOW. *Shroud Representing the Dormition of the Virgin.*   p. 146

Embroidery was one of the oldest arts of Russia, with traditions going back many centuries. Among its varied uses were embroidered shrouds made to hang below the icons on the iconostasis (i.e., altar screen), covering the space between the icons and the floor. Monastery and grand-ducal workshops were the main centers of this art.

In the middle of the Hermitage shroud is depicted the Dormition of the Mother of God, with the twelve Apostles at either side. Immediately above, Christ is represented receiving her into heaven, and the accompanying inscription quotes a text from the canticle for the feast of the Virgin.

The Shroud is notable for the subtlety of its execution, the elegance of its draughtsmanship, and the refined colors in clear and rich tones; it is a magnificent example of liturgical embroidery. Its iconographic schema, style and technique are typical of the work of the Muscovite embroiderers who created so many masterpieces of " pictorial needlework."

ART OF MOSCOW. *Chalice.*   p. 147

The chalice is a church vessel used in the celebration of the Eucharistic liturgy. The gold chalice in the Hermitage collection is a masterpiece of Russian jeweling from the end of the 17th century. It is lavishly decorated with precious stones and multicolored enamel. Around the upper edge of the chalice and on the base are inscriptions in niello inlays regarding the chalice, stating that it was made by the artists of the Moscow Kremlin, and that it was commissioned by the Czar Feodor Alekseevich for the palace Church of the Divine Saviour.

The elegant inscriptions, the flowers and fruit executed in relief which decorate the surface of the chalice, as well as the medallions in painted enamel with pictures of saints and religious scenes—all these elements combined

144

15

ART OF MOSCOW
Shroud Representing the Dormition of the Virgin
Second half of the XV century
Silk, gold and silver threads, *kamka* (ancient silk adorned with arabesques), taffeta, linen, embroidery; 15½" x 15½"

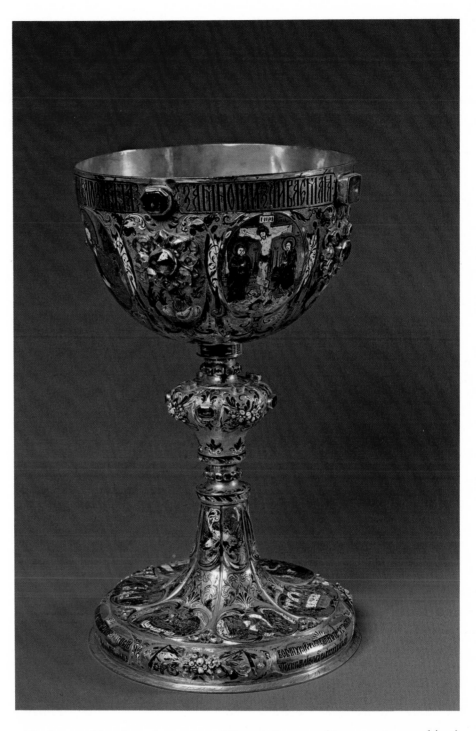

ART OF MOSCOW
Chalice
1677
Gold, precious stones, enamel, niello;
height 11½"; diameter 6⁹⁄₁₆"

with the sparkle of precious stones (diamonds, emeralds, garnets, sapphires) and the noble splendor of the polished gold surface create a vivid, festive range of colors.

Moscow gold- and silversmiths were famous; the best of them worked in the Kremlin workshops. The objects which they made were mainly for the Church: chalices, mitres, goblets, icon frames, missal mounts. They all have a strongly pronounced national character corresponding to the general trend of Russian art of that period with its predilection for bright polychrome and splendid decoration.

147

GRIGORY MUSIKISKY. *Portrait of Catherine I with*
Ekaterinhof in the background.

Catherine Alekseevna (1684–1727), daughter of Marta Skavronskaya (?), wife of Peter I, became Empress in 1725. Miniature portraits on enamel first appeared in Russia at the very beginning of the 18th century. The first artists to introduce them were G. Musikisky and A. Ovsov. Musikisky worked in the Moscow Armory, and then in 1711 moved to Petersburg. He

GRIGORY MUSIKISKY
1670–1671—after 1739
Portrait of Catherine I against a Background of
Ekaterinhof, 1724
Enamel on gold; 2⁹⁄₁₆″ x 3½″

IVAN VISHNIAKOV
Petersburg 1699—Petersburg 1761
Portrait of Stepanida Yakovleva
Oil on canvas; 35⁷⁄₁₆″ x 28⅜″

149

painted a large number of miniatures, mostly of Peter I—which the czar was accustomed to give as awards—and also many group portraits.

Musikisky was greatly influenced by traditional Russian enamelwork. He took the best characteristics of the old masters' work—the bright, festive colors, the naturalness and spontaneity—and managed to turn the miniature into an independent art form by bringing it closer to Russian painting and by improving on the old techniques. Among his best works are two imperial portraits—*Peter I, with the Peter and Paul Fortress in the background* and *Catherine I, with Ekaterinhof in the background.* (Ekaterinhof is a palace by the sea, near St. Petersburg.) Both of these miniatures were apparently painted to celebrate the twentieth anniversary of the founding of the new Russian capital.

Catherine's portrait is an interesting composition, an unusual interpretation of a known work by J. Nattier. The artist used an engraving of Ekaterinhof by A. Rostovtsev for the background. The colors are bold and clear.

IVAN VISHNIAKOV. *Portrait of Stepanida Yakovleva.*   *p. 149*

For a long time the portraits of the young merchant M. Yakovlev and his wife Stepanida (1742–1781) remained the work of an unknown artist. However, research carried out in the Hermitage and in the laboratories of the Russian Museum has enabled experts to establish the authorship of these two beautiful works. They are now attributed to I. Vishniakov, one of the leading Russian artists of the first half of the 18th century. Vishniakov was active in St. Petersburg in the years 1730–1750 as a decorator, teacher and portrait painter. He headed a large group of artists, the so-called "Art Group," which was responsible for the decoration of numerous palaces and churches in St. Petersburg. Today there remain in existence only a very few known signed works by Vishniakov. The Yakovlevs' portraits were painted in the late 1750s, not long after the couple's marriage.

Stepanida Yakovleva's portrait deserves particular attention. She is wearing a lovely light-colored dress woven with silk and gold thread, with bright diamonds in her hair and earrings. The young woman's pose—which clearly shows she is not used to sitting for an artist—is rather strained. Her graceful face stands out against the dark background. The atmosphere of Russian 17th century art can be distinctly felt in this portrait, with its lavish sense of decoration, the echoes of Russia's links abroad in the 17th and 18th centuries, and the rather flat quality of the picture, with its bright, rich tones and the abundance of ornamental accessories.

SAILING-SHIP CUP, 1706.   *p. 151*

The Hermitage possesses a large collection of silver objects made by Russian artists. Not only does this collection include household objects such as tableware, tureens, snuff boxes, etc.; it also has objects of a purely decorative nature, such as ceremonial ladles, cups, and trays, which for the most part were created to commemorate historical events. For example, this cup in the shape of a little boat was made from the first Russian silver mined in the region of Nerchinsk in 1706. Made in the shape of a single-masted warship, this interesting silver memento is reminiscent of the development of nautical pursuits and geological exploration in Russia at the beginning of the 18th century and was probably intended as a gift for Peter I.

150

SAILING-SHIP CUP
1706
Silver; welded, forged, chased, gilt;
length 12"
This curious piece of silver, which probably commemorated both the development of Russian navigation at the beginning of the XVIII century and geological exploration in Russia, was made as a gift to Peter I.

NICOLAI VERESHCHAGIN
ca. 1770–1814
Vase, 1798
Carved ivory; 33″ x 9⅞″ x 9⅞″

NICOLAI VERESHCHAGIN. *Vase.*

Among the various examples of Russian applied art, articles made of carved ivory by Northern Russian artists occupy a special place. The largest centers of carved ivory art were Kholmogory and Arkhangelsk, as well as neighboring villages. The Hermitage collection numbers over a thousand works of art made of carved ivory: caskets, goblets, vases, dressing-cases and little boxes, snuffboxes, combs, chess sets.

Nicolai Vereshchagin was the most famous practitioner of this art in the 18th and 19th centuries. The vase shown here is one of a pair made by him, and is typical of the traditional Russian art of ivory-carving. Vereshchagin's works are notable for their minutely fastidious interpretation of classical forms created like works of jewelry, as well as for their delicacy of ornament and the elegance of details in relief.

This vase is unequaled in the beauty of its outline and masterful execution. Here, the technique of pierced intaglio is employed with consummate virtuosity. The vase and its matching piece were intended as presents for the Emperor of Japan. But the diplomatic mission never took place, and the vases, having gone round the world between 1803 and 1806, finally returned to the Hermitage where they continue to impress visitors.

SEMYON SHCHEDRIN. *The Great Pond in Tsarskoye Selo Park.*

pp. 154–155

The work of Semyon Shchedrin, the distinguished landscapist of the second half of the 18th century, introduces us to the first native landscape painting in Russian art. Shchedrin painted views of the parks near St. Petersburg: Tsarskoye Selo, Peterhof, Pavlovsk and Gatchina. A student at the St. Petersburg Academy of Fine Arts and later the founder and for many years the head of its landscape-painting class, he became a true poet of the Russian countryside. The Hermitage collection possesses six views of Tsarskoye Selo Park, all painted in 1777. They were completed on royal commission and have been part of the museum collection since the 18th century.

The views of Tsarskoye Selo are painted in opaque color, consisting of gouache and white lead. The best of the series is *The Great Pond in Tsarskoye Selo Park.* The ingeniously raised foreground, the skillfully grouped trees and bushes, and the view stretching into the far distance give the composition a decorative air. The colors are a subtle combination of blue and green tones.

VOLOKITINO WARE. *Teapot and Teapot Warmer.*   *p. 156*

Teapots such as this one, resting on a pedestal inside which the spirit lamp was placed, began to appear in Russia in the first three decades of the 19th century, and were the product of private porcelain factories. The bizarre shape, the relief decoration, the polychrome ornament and the *rocaille* gilt are characteristic elements of the porcelain style called the "Second Rococo," dating from the 1840s and 1850s. The small round apertures on the sides of the pedestal provide the air for the lamp.

The output of the Miklashevsky factory is notable for the high quality and richness of its production. The factory was founded in 1839 in the village of Volokitino, in the province of Chernigov, in close proximity to the famous kaolin deposits of Glukhov which were used by many Russian porcelain factories, including the Imperial factory. The construction of the factory is linked with the name of the famous French ceramist Darte who lived a long time in Russia, and in the 1840s established new furnaces in the factory of the Kornilov brothers in St. Petersburg, and subsequently in the State factory.

Articles from the Miklashevsky factory found a large market in major Russian towns and the best ones went to the Imperial Palace. In the all-Russian artistic and industrial exhibition of 1849, china from the Miklashevsky factory won the gold medal.

Pp. 154–155
SEMYON SHCHEDRIN
St. Petersburg 1745—St. Petersburg 1804
The Great Pond in Tsarskoye Selo Park, 1777
Gouache over India ink outline drawing, on paper mounted on pale blue cardboard; signed and dated at lower right: *"S. Chedrin 1777"*

153

VOLOKITINO WARE
Teapot and Teapot Warmer
Mid-XIX century
Porcelain, painted and gilt relief ornament;
height 9⅞"
Produced by the Miklashevsky factory; bearing
the mark of the Miklashevsky coat of arms and
inscribed: *"Manufacture de Wolokitino."*

IMPERIAL PORCELAIN FACTORY OF ST. PETERSBURG. *Vase with Russian Dance.*   *p. 157*

Decorative porcelain vases were manufactured on special commission in the Imperial factory, in order to adorn the rooms of the Winter Palace and private residences in St. Petersburg and the suburbs; they were also used as gifts to diplomats and guests of high standing.

156   The most prevalent type of decoration on nineteenth-century vases became

IMPERIAL PORCELAIN FACTORY
OF ST. PETERSBURG
Vase with Russian Dance
Ca. 1810
Porcelain, obsidian; painted and gilt decoration
in relief; height 23⁷⁄₁₆"

what is known as the "pictorial" painting, consisting of copies of old master paintings, drawings, or etchings by Russian and foreign artists from the Hermitage collections.

On the front of this vase is a scene from popular life: a girl in a scarlet "sarafan" dress and a youth in a hat and tunic dance to the accompaniment of a lute and pipe. Under the picture is the signature of the artist, Golov, painter for the Imperial porcelain factory. A drawing called *Russian Dance* by E. Karneev, a professor of painting at the St. Petersburg Academy of Fine Arts, served as a model for the painting. The painter of the vase altered the format of the drawing and many details were omitted, but the characters have acquired classic proportions.

ALEKSEI VENETSIANOV
Moscow 1780—Poddub'e (Tver') 1847
Portrait of Mikhail Fonvizin
Pastel on parchment; 20¼" x 16¼"
Dated lower left: *"Le 3 Juin 1812"*

ALEKSEI VENETSIANOV. *Portrait of Mikhail Fonvizin.*

Aleksei Venetsianov, one of the leading Russian genre painters in the early 19th century, and the first to depict the feudal way of life in the Russian countryside at the time of the serfs, was also an excellent portrait painter.

The portrait of Fonvizin is one of the artist's best works. He portrayed the young man with an open, honest face expressing an inner purity, a poetic spirituality, chastity and seriousness. In his attempt to discover the inner personality of the sitter, Venetsianov omits anything extraneous to the subject. The attitude of the young man is reserved, the background neutral. Extremely simple in composition and with a remarkable harmony of color, Fonvizin's portrait is a superb example of 19th-century Russian realism.

Mikhail Fonvizin (1788–1853) was one of the most active participants in the Decembrist movement. At the time of the uprising of December 14, 1825, he was an official with a long record of service, having fought against Sweden and Napoleonic France. Following the defeat of the uprising, Fonvizin was sentenced to twelve years hard labor in Siberia. To the end of his days he remained a staunch opponent of czarism and serfdom. The strength of his convictions was combined with rare gifts of kindness and humanity.

LAPIDARY WORKS OF ST. PETERSBURG. *Malachite Vase.*   p. 160

Russia has long been famous for its lapidary art. Perfect taste and a high level of craftsmanship are typical of the gifted stonecarvers of St. Petersburg, the Urals and Siberia.

Among the rich collections of decorative stone objects in the Hermitage, the works in malachite hold a special place. The collection comprises over two hundred pieces which vary in shape and purpose, from monumental decorative vases to small decorative sculptures. One of the rooms of the Winter Palace, appropriately called the "Malachite Room," is entirely devoted to works in this mineral.

The most flourishing period of the production of malachite objects dates from the 1830s and 1840s. They are often decorated with gilt bronze, which heightens the noble beauty of the stone.

The vase illustrated here is a magnificient example of the decorative furniture in the Palace. The patterned composition of the stone is perfect, the silhouette of sophisticated beauty. The handles and applied decorations are executed in gilt bronze.

P. 160
LAPIDARY WORKS OF
ST. PETERSBURG
Malachite Vase
Ca. 1830
Malachite and gilt bronze; 26½" x 13⅛" x 13¼"
Peterhof workshop of hardstone carving near St. Petersburg.

159